Literature-Based Mini-Lessons

to Teach Decoding and Word Recognition

15 Engaging Lessons That Use Your Favorite Picture Books to Help Every Student Become a More Fluent Reader

by Susan Lunsford

NEW YORK • TORONTO • LONDON • AUCKLAND • SYDNEY
MEXICO CITY • NEW DELHI • HONG KONG

*With thanks to all the
children who have shared
their love of reading with me.*

May they enjoy a lifetime of happy reading!

FIRST GRADE READER

CREDITS

"Hug O' War" from *Where the Sidewalk Ends* by Shel Silverstein.
Copyright © 1974 by Evil Eye Music, Inc. Used with the permission of HarperCollins Publishers.

"Bleezer's Ice Cream" from *New Kid on the Block* by Jack Prelutsky.
Copyright © 1984 by Jack Prelutsky. Orginally published by Greenwillow Books. Used by permission of HarperCollins Publishers.

Scholastic grants teachers permission to photocopy the reproducible pages for classroom use only. No other part of this publication may be reproduced in whole or in part, or stored in a retrieval system, or transmitted in any form by any means, electronic, mechanical, photocopy, recording, or otherwise, without written permission of the publisher. For information regarding permission, write to Scholastic Professional Books, 555 Broadway, New York, NY 10012.

Cover and interior design by Kathy Massaro

Cover photo and photos on pages 10, 23, 39, 45, 59, 68, 86, 88, 95,
117, and 124 by Bruce Cramer of Cramer Studio.

Photo on page 154 by Oi Pin Chan.

All other photos courtesy of the author.

Illustrations by Rusty Fletcher.

ISBN 0-439-08682-5
Copyright © 2000 by Susan Lunsford
All Rights Reserved

Contents

Acknowledgments 5
Author's Note 6
Introduction 8

CHAPTER 1

True Clues: Rhyming Words 10

MINI-LESSON 1 ✷ The Magic of Rhyming Words
Goal: To explore rhyming words 11

MINI-LESSON 2 ✷ From Bats to Cats
Goal: To make new words by changing beginning letters 19

MINI-LESSON 3 ✷ Nonsense Rhyming Words
Goal: To invent rhyming words 27

Word Power Assessment 33

Books to Use 38

CHAPTER 2

Words With Happy Endings 39

MINI-LESSON 4 ✷ Mouses or Mice?
Goal: To explore plural endings 40

MINI-LESSON 5 ✷ Working With Words
Goal: To investigate words with -ing endings 48

MINI-LESSON 6 ✷ Laughed, Giggled and Grinned!
Goal: To investigate words with -ed endings 53

Word Power Assessment 61

Books to Use 67

CHAPTER 3

Snowballs, Gingerbread, and Other Special Words 68

MINI-LESSON 7 ✸ Snowballs, Gingerbread, and Rainbows
Goal: To examine compound words 69

MINI-LESSON 8 ✸ The Grouchy Ladybug's Blends
Goal: To identify words with initial consonant blends of r, s, and l 75

MINI-LESSON 9 ✸ Give Me a Break!
Goal: To separate words into syllables 82

Word Power Assessment 89
Books to Use 94

CHAPTER 4

Planting a Rainbow of Long and Short Vowels 95

MINI-LESSON 10 ✸ The Rainbow Rule
Goal: To examine the long vowel rule: when two vowels are together, the first vowel is long 96

MINI-LESSON 11 ✸ The Five Little Monkeys' Bossy E Rule
Goal: To examine words that follow the silent e long vowel rule 103

MINI-LESSON 12 ✸ Max, Fox, Henry, Mudge and the Little Critters' Short Vowel Sounds
Goal: To investigate words with short vowel sounds 109

Word Power Assessment 118
Books to Use 123

CHAPTER 5

Extending and Reviewing Word Power Skills 124

MINI-LESSON 13 ✸ Same Words, Different Meanings, Same Meanings, Different Words
Goal: To investigate homonyms and synonyms 125

MINI-LESSON 14 ✸ A Noun Pizza
Goal: To identify a noun as a person, place, or thing 133

MINI-LESSON 15 ✸ Review With Yoko
Goal: To review word power skills 140

Word Power Assessment 146
Books to Use 153

Appendix: Book Lists 154

Acknowledgments

There's something special about the feel of a new book in your hands—opening the cover for the first time after examining it for details, anticipating what may occur on the upcoming pages. Books are full of excitement, and when you feel this excitement for literature, the children you teach will feel it too.

As a child, I knew I wanted to help other children learn how to read and love books so that they could experience E.B. White's *Charlotte's Web*, Kenneth Grahame's *The Wind in the Willows*, and Maurice Sendak's *Where the Wild Things Are*. A love of children's literature is one of the main reasons I became a teacher "when I grew up." Teachers have the opportunity every day to share the gift of reading books with others.

I have written this book to share my enthusiasm for children's literature with other teachers so that they might explore the world of reading in new and exciting ways with students. The following people made it possible for me to share the ideas in this book with you, and I offer them my thanks.

To my father, for his support of my love of reading as a child by always buying "just one more book" from the school book club when my bookshelf was already overflowing, but most especially for his constant support of "me."

To my husband, Brad, and my son, Ryan, for understanding when I needed "just one more hour" of uninterrupted writing time, "just one more trip" to the bookstore, and "just one more night" of delivered pizza.

To Cindy Cowan and Susan Feldman for allowing me to share my ideas with them, for sharing their beginning readers with me, and most of all, for their friendship.

To the children at Ferguson Elementary for sharing their excitement for literature, their favorite books, and their ideas about the world of words with me.

Author's Note

The Book Time Approach

Within the realm of most primary classrooms, like my own multi-age group of first and second graders, there is a range of reading abilities, from the pre-reader who sounds out each letter in a word, to the beginning reader who reads simple sentences, to the fluent reader who reads chapter books with expression and understanding. Given the diversity of readers and their individual needs, teachers often struggle with how to best organize instructional reading time to allow for:

- small group reading instruction
- whole class meetings to teach skills
- independent practice of skills learned
- independent reading of self-selected books
- activities that extend and celebrate books read

Having tried many different approaches to incorporate these elements into my daily reading program, I developed what has come to be known as Book Time in my classroom. Book Time begins with a literature-based "word power" mini-lesson for the whole class. These lessons are designed to build an awareness of the kinds of words students will encounter and to develop strategies for reading these words.

A young reader enjoys a favorite book during silent reading time.

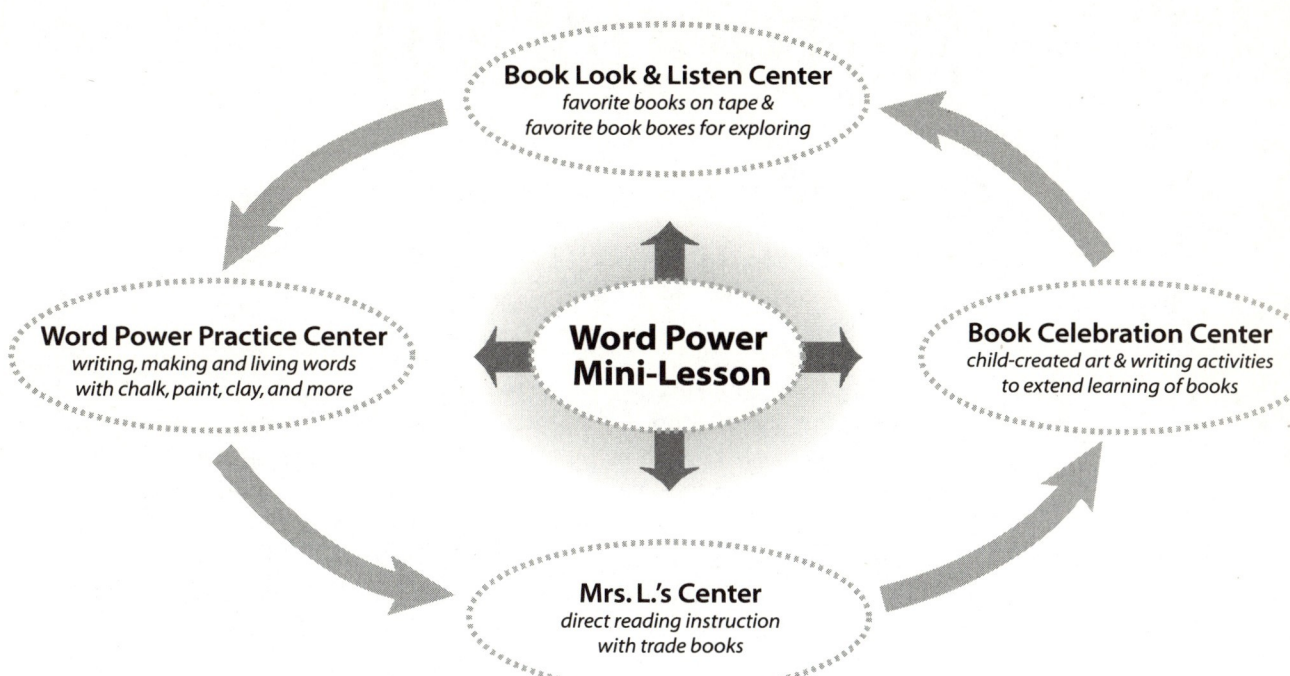

The mini-lesson is just one integral part of the overall reading program and encourages readers to think about words. Any given word power lesson may be review for some students while it is the introduction of a skill for others; each lesson benefits all students by exposing them to the world of words using authentic children's literature.

To apply our mini-lesson topics and ensure a balanced reading program, I incorporated four centers, or work stations, into our Book Time. Students spend the hour following the mini-lesson working for 15 minutes at each center on activities that extend their understanding of words and develop strategies to make them more successful readers.

At the end of Book Time each day, students have had

1. a full group, literature-based mini-lesson on a word study skill of interest to young readers.
2. small group, teacher-directed reading instruction using multiple copies of trade books.
3. independent practice of word skills using a variety of mediums.
4. time for selecting and reading books independently or with a parent volunteer.
5. time to extend the enjoyment of books read through art and creative writing activities.

Experiment with the mini-lessons in this book and adapt them to fit your students' needs and your teaching style. Use some lessons for your whole class, others for small group instruction. Then examine your reading program to see if it provides a variety of different activities to get your students excited about books— the only way to get your students *reading happily ever after.*

Introduction

Magically, it happens...

I remember I was sitting in my favorite chair in our living room when it happened. I was looking at my new book from the school book club when, with a great deal of effort, I deciphered the words on one whole page of text all by myself. I ran, beaming with pride, to tell my father the news—*I could READ!* This newly found ability opened up a whole world for me—from reading cereal boxes to road signs. I was now a reader and could make sense of the world of words.

As a teacher, I've often heard parents of beginning readers explain how their children magically one day could read. I think these children, like me, have had the desire to read; when immersed in an environment of books and given encouragement and patience for their efforts, they do seemingly become readers overnight, like magic. In actuality, this reading fluency has developed gradually over time. Even knowing this, I began to wish I could capture this magic and bring it to my Book Time mini-lessons that introduce word power skills. That's how my idea for this book began.

I had seen success with my literature-based writing workshop mini-lessons (see my book *Literature-Based Mini-Lessons to Teach Writing*, Scholastic Professional Books, 1998). Using works of expert authors as models for writing gave my beginning writers greater enthusiasm, confidence, and pride with regard to their writing accomplishments. Once again I turned to the authors of children's literature, this time for planning mini-lessons that would help my beginning readers develop strategies for decoding unknown words, which would, in turn, improve their reading confidence. Most importantly I was optimistic that these expert authors, with their books kids can't wait to read again and again, would help my students see the value of learning to read by encouraging a love of literature.

To begin, I introduced favorite author Jack Prelutsky to my classroom with his book *The New Kid on the Block* and quickly discovered that *cocoa mocha macaroni* and *tapioca smoked baloney*, from the poem "Bleezer's Ice Cream," make a more lasting impression of rhyming word pairs than does merely brainstorming lists of rhyming words. On another day, while reading Eric Carle's *The Grouchy Ladybug*, I noticed more than 25 words with initial consonant blends—among them *flippers*, *screeched*, and *stinger*, not to mention *grouchy*. When it was time for a lesson on reading consonant blends, the students listened to this story again, this time armed with lap-sized chalkboards and chalk to record words with *r-*, *s-* and *l-*blends. Similarly, *Mouse Mess* by Linnea Riley became the book used to identify words with plural endings *-s* and *-es*, for such words abound within the pages of this mouse's mess. I found that the books my students and I loved and read over and over also showcased the kinds of words I wanted to study in my word power lessons.

Every book deemed a favorite by my class is placed in our Favorite Books Box, and I recycle them for Book Time mini-lessons. Once a word power skill is identified through student reading conferences, independent reading, or direct reading instruction time, I search the box for examples of each particular kind of word. By bringing these favorite books to a mini-lesson and focusing on skills all fluent readers must possess, my beginning readers see that once they master a word power strategy, their new word knowledge can help them decode many other new words.

While the lessons in this book use my favorites, you can substitute your own—the only requirement is that you and your students know and love the books. After reading favorite books together for pleasure, turn to them again to examine the words used to tell the story. Reusing these books written by expert authors who "play with words" on a daily basis makes the exploration of word study skills more fun for young readers and helps prove each skill's relevance to the "real world" of words.

Arming your students with word study strategies learned from the pages of their favorite literature will give them reading confidence. With confidence and enthusiasm for reading, children run as quickly to the library as they do out to recess and are as excited when book orders arrive as they are when it's time to open presents. You will see your students thrilled to discover a new book has been published by their favorite author. A love of literature gives students the desire to learn to read, which is the first step toward becoming fluent, lifelong readers.

The Favorite Books Box: Our collection of favorite books is kept in one convenient place, ready at a moment's notice for a literature-based mini-lesson.

CHAPTER 1
True Clues: Rhyming Words

Mini-Lessons

The Magic of Rhyming Words

From Bats to Cats

Nonsense Rhyming Words

Student Goals

To explore rhyming words

To make new words by changing beginning letters

To invent rhyming words

Favorite Books to Use

The New Kid on the Block by Jack Prelutsky
Feathers for Lunch by Lois Ehlert
Chicka Chicka Boom Boom by Bill Martin Jr. and John Archambault
Something Big Has Been Here by Jack Prelutsky
17 Kings and 42 Elephants by Margaret Mahy
Miss Spider's Tea Party by David Kirk

The Magic of Rhyming Words

GOAL To explore rhyming words

Our introduction to rhyming words usually begins with one of the many poems by Jack Prelutsky or Shel Silverstein that I share with children. After sharing and charting a few poems, strictly for their sheer silliness or the way they relate to a particular theme or event in our school day, I use the poems as a springboard for teaching certain reading and writing skills, such as rhyming words. Since the children love saying the poems over and over again, I never hear complaints as we reread a few poems looking for rhyming words.

An added dimension of playfulness occurs with poems as kids mimic the language and the obvious beat of the reading. Although rhymes are simple to identify for avid readers, I am always amazed by how many beginning readers do not understand what makes a rhyme. After this initial lesson on exploring rhyming word pairs, children are better equipped for explaining the concept of rhyme, and they begin to use rhyme to decode words that differ from words they know by only the beginning sounds.

When Jonathan, a most active, "challenging child," asked if he could use his recess time to copy "Bleezer's Ice Cream," all 28 flavors, so he could read it to his grandmother, I knew I needed to bring this excitement to a mini-lesson on rhyming words. The motivation is built-in since identifying rhyming words is especially fun when you're talking about pickles, pumpernickel, bubble gum, and plums. Be on the lookout for such student favorites; they automatically become candidates for future word power mini-lessons because of their strong kid appeal.

The lesson that introduces rhyming words to my beginning readers usually goes something like this:

BLEEZER'S ICE CREAM

I am Ebenezer Bleezer,
I run BLEEZER'S ICE CREAM STORE,
there are flavors in my freezer
you have never seen before,
twenty-eight divine creations
too delicious to resist,
why not do yourself a favor,
try the flavors on my list:

Cocoa Mocha Macaroni
Tapioca Smoked Baloney
Checkerberry Cheddar Chew
Chicken Cherry Honeydew
Tutti-Fruitti Stewed Tomato
Tuna Taco Baked Potato
Lobster Litchi Lima Bean
Mozzarella Mangosteen
Almond Ham Meringue Salami
Yam Anchovy Prune Pastrami
Sassafras Souvlaki Hash
Sukiyaki Succotash…

—from *The New Kid on the Block*
by Jack Prelutsky, page 48.

Mrs. L.:	Today I want to show you a reading magic trick. To help me with the trick, I have copied one of our favorite poems on this chart.
Greg:	"Bleezer's Ice Cream," I bet.
Tommy:	By Jack Prelutsky.
Mrs. L.:	What is it about Jack Prelutsky's poems that makes us want to read them over and over again?
Marc:	"Bleezer's Ice Cream" is fun to say because of the silly words.
Tommy:	Yes, like *cocoa mocha macaroni*.
Bobby:	There are tongue twisters in some of them.
Mrs. L.:	I agree. Tell me more.
Abbey:	They have a beat you can clap and that's fun too.
Allisa:	I like them because you can figure out what comes next because the words give you hints.
Olivia:	Even though sometimes the words are so crazy, they don't make sense.
Carrie:	Like having baloney in your ice cream—YUK! But he had to write *baloney* because it goes with the other word.
Katie:	*Macaroni*.
Mrs. L.:	I see. *Baloney* goes with *macaroni*.
Bobby:	They both end with the "eee" sound.
Mrs. L.:	Can you find another pair of words like that?
Sara:	How about the *tomato-potato* one. They both have *ato* in them.
Mrs. L.:	Good remembering. Do you know what we call words that end with the same letter sounds?
Jonathan:	Yes, rhymes. That's what makes them poems.
Mrs. L.:	You're right. But not all poems rhyme. It just so happens that most of Jack Prelutsky's poems do rhyme, and that's probably one of the reasons we like them so much. Can you tell me how knowing about rhyming words might help us be better readers?
David:	Well, you can figure out a word if it looks almost just like another word. You know the way *cluster* and *bluster* look almost the same. Only the *c* and *b* are different.
Mrs. L.:	Yes, it's like magic! If you can read *c-luster*, you can read *b-luster*. Once you can read and remember a part of one word, you can read other words with that part, too—like *luster* and *buster*. Let's circle the words at the end of each line in "Bleezer's Ice Cream" and see what we discover. I'll circle *macaroni* and *baloney* first.
Anna:	You should underline the part that is the same sound too.
Mrs. L.:	Good idea.
Stephanie:	It sounds like *e*, but they don't have *e*'s at the end.
Greg:	They must not be rhyming words.
Mrs. L.:	Well, words don't have to look alike to be rhyming words. They can sound alike, all but the beginning letter, and that's what makes them rhyming words.

Sara:	So it must be the *o-n-i* in *macaroni* and the *o-n-e-y* in *baloney* because those parts that sound alike start with *o*.
Mrs. L.:	Great. I'll write *macaroni* and *baloney* on this side of the chart. I'll label these words "Sound-Alike Rhyming Words" since they sound alike but the parts that sound alike are spelled differently. What's next?
Tommy:	*Chew* and *honeydew*. That's easier. They both have *ew*.
Allisa:	They look alike and sound alike.
Mrs. L.:	I'll label this pair "Look-and-Sound-Alike Rhyming Words."
Greg:	Then there's *tomato* and *potato*.
Stephanie:	They look and sound alike.
Mrs. L.:	Right. I'll write them under "Look-and-Sound-Alike." What's next?
Alex:	*Mangosteen* and *bean*. I bet it's *e-e-n* and *e-a-n*. Am I right?
Mrs. L.:	That's the part that makes the *een* sound, as far as I know.
Carrie:	*Pastrami* and *salami* are next. They're easy too. *Ami* and *ami*.
Mrs. L.:	You're getting very good at this! Let's try a few more. Then we'll put the poem back together and practice reading the rhyming word lists.

Look-and-Sound-Alike Rhyming Words

dew and chew
tomato and potato
salami and pastrami
hash and succotash
plum and bubble gum
bluster and cluster
custard and mustard
dip and flip
guava and lava

Sound-Alike Rhyming Words

macaroni and baloney
bean and mangosteen
pickle and pumpernickel
sprout and sauerkraut
beet and wheat

Although the children may not become poets after our initial lesson on rhyming words, they all benefit from exploring how these words work. On another day, I display the chart shown at right.

Seeing the rhyming words in a lengthy list makes an impression on beginning readers who may now realize a very helpful reading clue. On other days we choose a different word and brainstorm more rhyming words.

MANAGEMENT TIP

Asking students to name their favorite flavor of Bleezer's ice cream allows you to discuss rhyming word pairs at random as opposed to reading down the list in the poem. This approach keeps students from anticipating what rhyming pairs will be discussed next.

Book Celebrations: Activities to Extend Learning

Act It Out

After the children learn the poem "Bleezer's Ice Cream" nearly by heart, we set up our own class ice cream store and dramatize this favorite poem. The students work together to decorate a refrigerator box to look like Bleezer's Ice Cream stand. Next we decide which student will play the part of Ebenezer Bleezer. Depending on the number of interested actors, we hold tryouts to decide who reads the part with the greatest expression in his or her voice. This person makes the "best salesperson."

We then decide who orders which delicious flavor. To do this, I copy onto slips of paper enough flavors from the poem to match the number of students and place the papers in a hat. (For example, with 22 students, I write the names of the first 22 flavors from the poem on slips of paper.) After students decorate paper ice cream cones to look like their chosen flavors, we line up in front of the decorated ice cream stand in the order Bleezer's flavors are listed in the poem ("cocoa mocha macaroni" is first in line, "tapioca smoked baloney" is second in line, and so on).

With the list of specials hanging on the wall, the students take turns ordering a cone by reciting their chosen flavor from the poem. Mr. Bleezer hands each customer a paper cone and the customer takes a quick lick before getting back in line for more. When the first student in line is ready to order again, he or she keeps the poem moving along by ordering the next flavor on the list. We continue in this manner until all 28 flavors have been named and Mr. Bleezer can give his ending lines: "I am Ebenezer Bleezer. I run Bleezer's Ice Cream Store. Taste a flavor from my freezer you will surely ask for more." The students usually ask for more time for this activity!

Two tasty ice cream cones

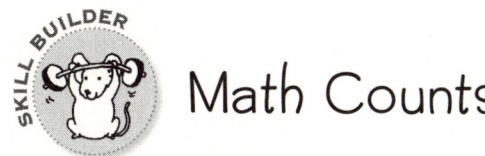

Math Counts

During independent work times, students may take turns buying and selling ice cream cones from Bleezer's Ice Cream Store. Using plastic quarters, nickels, dimes, and pennies as well as our cardboard storefront and paper ice cream cones, students practice buying cones and making change. The customers must keep in mind that Bleezer often will try to trick them into receiving the wrong change!

Make Ice Cream

As a culmination to our "Bleezer's Ice Cream" celebration, we make homemade ice cream on a Friday afternoon. I write the recipe for "Bleezer's Plain Old Ordinary Vanilla Ice Cream" on the board (see my recipe below). After a quick lesson on measuring, we mix the rather ordinary ingredients. While the students copy the recipe on a recipe card to take home, the ice cream churns in my electric ice cream maker. Parents provide toppings of chocolate, whipped cream, crushed cookies, candies, cherries and nuts*. The children add their imagination, of course, as they pretend to enjoy "tuna taco baked potato" and "lobster litchi lima bean," just to name a few delectable flavors.

Bleezer's Plain Old Ordinary Vanilla Ice Cream

- 2 cups whipping cream
- 2 cups half-and-half
- 1 cup sugar
- 1 tablespoon vanilla extract

1. Mix all ingredients in ice cream container.
2. Stir until the sugar is dissolved.
3. Place container in electric ice cream machine.
4. Follow the directions for your ice cream machine.

---

* Be sure to check with parents about any possible food allergies your students might have.

Mini Ice Cream Books

I was delighted when several students asked for time to copy the poem "Bleezer's Ice Cream" from our class chart but worried that the time and energy required of first- and second-grade students to copy the lengthy poem would lead to frustration. So I developed a cloze activity that lends a hand in copying the poem (see pages 35 and 36). An illustrated ice cream cone decorates the cover, and additional blank pages allow for flexibility in copying all or part of Ebenezer's menu, depending on a child's interest. You may wish to provide patterns to assist students in making an ice-cream–shaped booklet. Students take the completed booklets home to their families and benefit from the extra reading practice required of sharing the poem again and again and again!

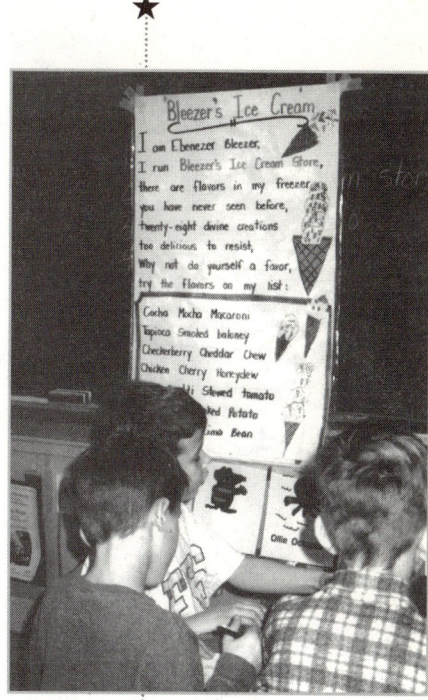

Making ice cream books ▶

More Food Fun: Grasshopper Gumbo

"Grasshopper gumbo, iguana tail tarts, toad à la mode, pickled pelican parts…" So begins the poem "Grasshopper Gumbo" by Jack Prelutsky (*Something Big Has Been Here*, page 52). After revealing in the last line that "the school cafeteria serves them [such dishes] for lunch," the students giggle with delight and beg to memorize this poem with a strong rhyming beat.

The students enjoy making bowls of clay grasshopper gumbo or plates of toad à la mode. Using plastic bowls and plates, each child chooses a favorite line from the poem, or invents an original culinary creation, then forms colored clay to make a sample menu item.

The table is set for "Grasshopper Gumbo." ▶

Write a Letter to Mr. Bleezer

Inside our Bleezer's Ice Cream Store, as in every reputable business concerned about its customers, there is a suggestion box. I explain to the students that Mr. Bleezer wants to make sure his customers are happy and enjoys receiving comments and suggestions for making his store better. During independent work time, I invite these young "customers" to write notes to Mr. Bleezer, telling him their thoughts about his unusual ice cream store. The students are anxious to jot down a few lines—some suggesting, others complaining—and then place the index card of ideas into the shoe-box suggestion box.

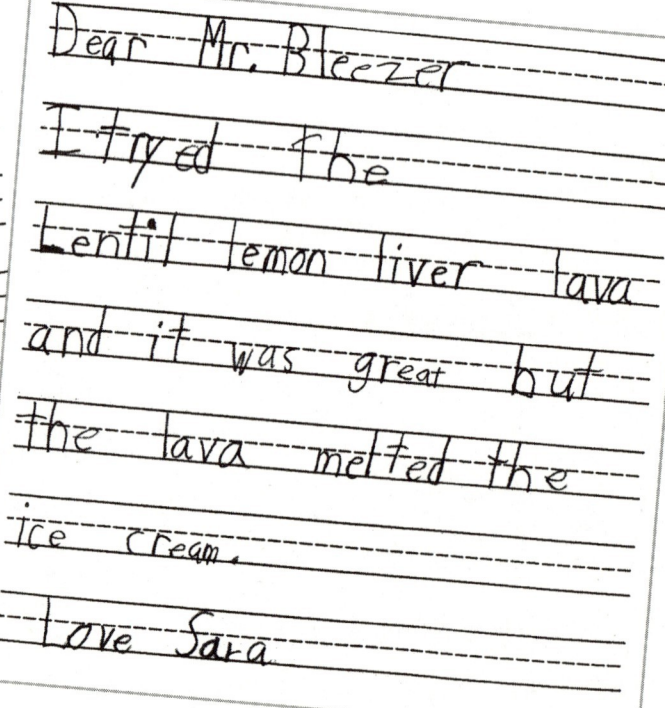

Dear Mr. Bleezer...

From Bats to Cats

GOAL To make new words by changing beginning letters

In the previous lesson, kids explored how rhymes worked by reading a poem and examining rhyming pairs. Now we explore a new poem, this time using the rhyming pairs to generate our own rhyming words. In this way, kids learn about word families and get practice using rhyme as a decoding tool.

Lois Ehlert's Feathers for Lunch *is a book with many uses in a primary classroom. It inspires children to illustrate with collage and write adventure stories about natural enemies and also proves helpful on a class bird walk or for reports on special birds. Using this book as a springboard for a lesson on rhyming words happens to be one of my favorite activities.*

I prepare for this mini-lesson by charting the text of the story in poem form so that all the words are on one chart, making it easily viewed for discussion. Next, I arrange magnetic alphabet letters on my white board in alphabetical order. After briefly reviewing the poem for "look-alike" and "sound-alike" rhyming word pairs (see the previous lesson on rhyming words), the students and I discover whole families of words just by changing beginning letters.

Feathers for Lunch by Lois Ehlert, 1990 ▶

MANAGEMENT TIP

If your blackboard or white board is not magnetic, try placing sticky tack on the back of foam or other alphabet letters and attaching them to the board. Or make a transparency of the Alphabet Fun Letters on page 37 and then cut the letters into squares to manipulate on the overhead. Though a bit time-consuming, the extra work makes an effective visual aid.

Mrs. L.: I have copied the words from one of our favorite books onto this chart.

Class: *Feathers for Lunch!*

Allisa: It looks just like a poem.

Mrs. L.: Many rhyming-word books would look like poems if they were written this way. I bet Lois Ehlert wrote her story on paper like a poem before she added the illustrations. This makes it easier to see the rhyming word pairs. I am so impressed by the way Lois Ehlert tells the story in rhyme. This must have taken a great deal of work.

Jonathan: She must be a good rhymer.

Mrs. L.: I agree. She probably enjoys playing with words—thinking of words she can use to make her story sound just right.

David: I like the menu part. It's funny to think of a cat reading a menu!

Mrs. L.: Yes, it is. Maybe she thought of lunch words and menu came to mind, and then she thought of a word that rhymed with menu, and it was new so she came up with an idea that went along with her story. Why do you think she wanted *Feathers for Lunch* to be a rhyming book?

Sara: Rhyming makes it fun to read because the beat is fun.

Marc: And the story wouldn't have been as fun if she had just told a story about a cat that almost ate a bird but didn't. Since it rhymes you want to read it over and over and over again!

Allisa: And every time I read it, I see something new in the pictures.

Mrs. L.: Me too. I think the pictures help tell the story. Pictures and rhymes are helpful clues when you're reading.

Anna: You always tell us that good readers "read" the pictures before they read the words because pictures give you clues about the words in the story.

Mrs. L.: And rhyming word books help readers with words in another way. I was surprised at how quickly you figured out the word *warning*.

Carrie: It was with *morning* so the word had to be *warning*, even though it was *a-r* instead of *o-r*. They have to sound alike.

Matthew: If you were reading the book and got to *warning*, you might have to skip ahead to find out what word it rhymed with—until you saw *morning*.

Mrs. L.: Excellent! Since I copied this story like a poem, let's read the rhyming word pairs at the end of each line.

Class: Crack–back, new–menu, mild–wild, good–would, warning–morning, soar–for, munch–lunch.

Mrs. L.: There are many other words you can read just by knowing these rhyming word pairs.

Tommy: But not all books rhyme and that hint isn't always there.

Mrs. L.:	True, but if you remember how to read a chunk of a word, like *unch*, in the word *lunch*, all you have to do is substitute another sound at the beginning. Then there are a lot of other words you can read. Maybe you could help me play with these letters a bit. Let's pretend we have an assignment to help Lois Ehlert do word research for a new book. Our job is to help her think of rhyming words to go along with some words she used in *Feathers for Lunch*. To start, I'll spell *lunch* using the magnetic letters.
Billy:	You're making me hungry.
Mrs. L.:	Sorry. I'll take the *l* away. Is that better?
Class:	Yes!
Mrs. L.:	What do we have now?
Class:	*Unch.*
Mrs. L.:	Good. Now I'll bring one letter at a time from our magnetic ABC letters and place it in front of *unch*. Each time we make a word, we'll put it in this box I've drawn on the board. If the letter doesn't make a real *unch* word, I'll put it back at the top. Let me bring down the *a* and add it to *unch*. What do we have now?
Class:	*Aunch.*
Mrs. L.:	Is this a word?
Class:	No.
Mrs. L.:	Okay. Let's put the *a* back at the top and try again.
Bobby:	B will make a real word.
Mrs. L.:	B-u-n-c-h spells…
Class:	Bunch!
Sara:	C makes *cunch* and that's not a word.
Mrs. L.:	You're right. So *c* goes back at the top. What about *d*?
David:	*Dunch* is not a word, either.
Mrs. L.:	I don't think that's in the dictionary, is it? What about *e*?
Class:	No.
Mrs. L.:	F would be…

(We continue bringing down successive magnetic letters and adding them to *unch*, rejecting those letters that do not make a new word and putting those letters that do make a real word in our box. When we finish, our list of *unch* words includes *bunch*, *hunch*, *lunch*, *munch*, and *punch*. Next, we think of a few other words to add to our list.)

Mrs. L.:	Can you think of any blended sounds that can be added to *unch* to make a new word? I'm thinking of a word that also makes me hungry. It's not exactly breakfast, and it's not exactly lunch. It's a combination of the two meals.
Bobby:	Brunch!

Mrs. L.: Exactly! I'll add *brunch* to our list. What about a blended word that starts with *c* and is another way of describing the sound you make when you eat something with a hard texture?

Jonathan: *Cunch?*

Mrs. L.: Close. You need one more letter that blends with *c* to make a real *unch* word.

Carrie: *Crunch!*

Mrs. L.: Right! For now I think we're out of *unch* words. If you come across another *unch* word in your reading, we'll add it to our list.

Let's read the list of *Unch* Family Words:

Class:
Bunch
Hunch
Lunch
Munch
Punch
Brunch
Crunch

Mrs. L.: Great! I'll put the magnetic letters back in alphabetical order, and we'll try another word family.

(The class generates more families of words using the rhyming pairs from *Feathers for Lunch*.)

Mrs. L.: I think of these words that have a similar part as families of words. Members of a family have different first names but usually the same last names. Words can be thought of in the same way. Some words have different first letters but the rest of them are the same. Let's keep our eyes open for *unch* and *ack* family words. There may be other words to add to our list.

From now on, whenever you come to a word that causes you to trip, look for anything about that word that may look familiar. Does the word belong to a family that you have seen before? If it does, you have a great hint for helping you figure out that unknown word. Tomorrow, I'll give you a chance to make more rhyming word lists using your own set of alphabet letters.

Book Celebrations: Activities to Extend Learning

Exploring Rhyming Word Families With Alphabet Fun Letters

Use the Alphabet Fun Letters on page 37 to help your students explore rhyming word families. Pass out copies of this reproducible page and direct students to cut out the boxes and arrange them in alphabetical order across the tops of their desks. Students then choose a word family from the Word Families to Explore poster ideas below (*ew, or,* and *ild* are families from *Feathers for Lunch*; you can create your own chart from your favorite rhyming book). Offer the choice of working alone or in pairs to place one letter at a time in front of the chosen word ending. Letters that make real words are placed in a special part of the desk and reviewed after all letters have been tested.

At the end of the activity provide students with plastic bags for letter storage. You may wish to store all the bags in a small basket so they are not lost in the depths of student desks. Parent volunteers may make a few extra Alphabet Fun Letters for a Lost and Found Letter Bag to be used for replacing those letters which are bound to fall to the floor and be swept away.

WORD FAMILIES TO EXPLORE

-at, -in, -ean, -op, -ight, -or, -ew, -ild, -ill, -og, -un, -ack, -ate

Working with Alphabet Fun Letters

MANAGEMENT TIP

To make the Alphabet Fun Letters more durable, copy or have students glue copies of page 37 onto oak tag. To have the letters ready for a morning mini-lesson, post directions on the board for the students when they arrive and provide small plastic bags for the cut-out letters. This makes a great early morning activity for students and saves cutting time after the mini-lesson.

Words to Munch: Making Rhyming Word Books

Individual student-made rhyming word books titled *Words to Munch* motivate students to record families of words. Have students design a cover for the book in the shape of a cat or bird in honor of *Feathers for Lunch*, or have them design a cover for your favorite rhyming book. Place several blank sheets of paper inside for lists of rhyming words. Trim excess paper edges to match the cover shape. On blank pages inside, students record word lists they have made during independent time using Word Families to Explore and Alphabet Fun Letters.

For extra fun, invent a poem to be copied on the first page to introduce the book, such as the one in the following sample.

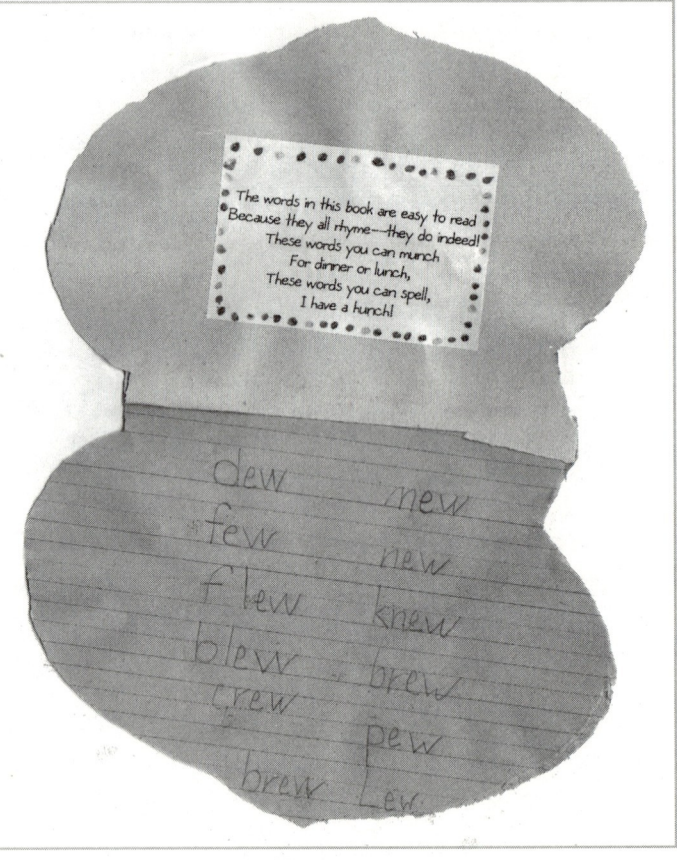

The words in this book are easy to read
Because they all rhyme—they do indeed!
These words you can munch,
for dinner or lunch.
These words you can spell,
I have a hunch!

Read It Again

Encourage your students to read a charted version of your favorite rhyming book in a variety of creative ways; each different reading reinforces word recognition. Suggest a pattern for the reading, such as girls reading one line followed by boys reading the next line, or one side of the room reading two lines followed by the other side of the room reading two lines. Have people wearing shoes with laces read a line and those with Velcro read the next—the possibilities are endless! For extra fun, you may wish to have actors take turns playing the characters as the rest of the class reads the narrator's part.

Clay Rhyming Words

Using Word Families to Explore and a tub of clay, students can have hands-on experience with rhyming words. Students select a word family such as -*at* and build these letters with clay (for younger children, you may wish to model how to make clay "snakes" to shape into letters). As done in the mini-lesson, they continue forming a different letter of the alphabet and adding it to -*at* to discover all the words in this family. Challenge students to experiment with adding blends to the word family before recording the new family of words in their *Words to Munch* recording books.

Hands-on experience with rhyming words ▶

Meet the Author

Take your students on a video visit to meet Lois Ehlert. The video titled *Color World* (Harcourt Brace & Company, 1994) takes viewers on a shopping trip to find fruit and vegetable models for *Eating the Alphabet* and introduces them to other book models, such as Buffy, the cat from *Feathers for Lunch*. Viewers will learn other Lois Ehlert secrets, such as the word hidden within the illustrations of *Fish Eyes*, the real-life story behind *Nuts to You*, and the card table from her childhood where she made her first creations. Lois Ehlert invites the audience into her studio, where she gives a demonstration of the painting and cutting techniques she uses to make her unique book illustrations. This video will inspire many young artists to give their illustrating techniques a try, so have lots of construction paper scraps and unusual objects ready so your students can make color worlds of their own!

Inspired by Lois Ehlert

◀ *One young illustrator's collage work*

Nonsense Rhyming Words

GOAL To invent rhyming words

In order to practice more with rhyming words and give kids confidence in rearranging words to help with decoding, I like to do a lesson on invented rhyming words. The mini-lesson that follows provides a fun way for students to manipulate words, to see how initial sounds affect words, and to play with language by inventing nonsense words of their own.

Chicka Chicka Boom Boom features rhyming language, nonsense words and a beat that makes it perfect for a lesson. I introduce the book by reading the story without ever turning the pages—from memory. I tell the class how Chicka Chicka Boom Boom was my son's first favorite book and how from reading it over and over again to him, I quickly memorized it. We talk about how rhyming poems and books are actually easy to memorize once you've found the beat and use the rhyming word clues. As you can imagine, my beginning readers are eager to practice this story repeatedly so that they can retell the story from memory just like me. After I read the book several times, emphasizing the beat while the children chime in on the chicka chicka boom boom *parts, we return to the book for a closer look at a few favorite lines and to invent some rhyming words of our own.*

Skit skat skoodle doot.
Flip flop flee.
Everybody running to the coconut tree...

—<u>Chicka Chicka Boom Boom</u>, page 13

Mrs. L.: I told you that when my son was ten months old, he would crawl over to his book basket and throw all the other books on the floor searching for *Chicka Chicka Boom Boom*. I probably read it to him five times a day for months! He had the baby-board book version, and I eventually had to get him a second copy because the first book was peeling apart from being read so much.

Carrie: It was a well-loved book!

27

Mrs. L.:	You're right! Then one day Ryan got very fussy in the car. To cheer him up, I started to say the words to the story while I was driving. He immediately started to smile and bounce and giggle in his car seat. When I said the lines *Skit skat skoodle doot* and *Flip flop flee*, which weren't in his board-book version but were lines I remembered from my own book, Ryan nearly fell out of his seat giggling. The words are fun to hear and say—*Skit skat skoodle doot. Flip flop flee.* Try it.
Class:	*Skit skat skoodle doot. Flip flop flee.*
Matthew:	It's almost like a tongue twister.
Mrs. L.:	Yes. And I bet John Archambault and Bill Martin Jr. brainstormed many different rhymes for this part before deciding on a favorite.
Matthew:	I bet they tried out ideas until they found one that sounded just right.
Mrs. L.:	I'd like to try playing with these words. I'll write *Skit skat skoodle doot. Flip flop flee* on the board in big letters. Then I'll erase the beginning sounds so we can invent some of our own words. Please read what we have now:
Class:	__ it __ at __ oodle __ oot. __ ip __op __ee.
Mrs. L.:	Right. This is the part that stays the same while the beginning letters change. Some of the words we think of today may not be real words—let's call them "nonsense words" because they won't make any sense. They will just be fun words that wouldn't be found in the dictionary. Let's invent some words that fit the beat and rhyme with *Skit skat scoodle doot. Flip flop flee.* All you need to do is name a letter or a blend that you think will sound fun with *it, at, oodle, oot, ip, op, ee.*
Abbey:	How about *bl*?
Mrs. L.:	Great! What would our new nonsense line become?
Abbey:	*Blit blat bloodle*, but the next word changes.
Mrs. L.:	Right. You are the writer. Please choose a new word.
Abbey:	Okay, *eoot*. Now the words change again.
Mrs. L.:	Any ideas?
David:	How about *zl*?
Mrs. L.:	Sure. That would make the next part:
Class:	*Zlip zlop zlee.*
Mrs. L.:	Let me write this down. The whole line is now:
Class:	*Blit blat bloodle eoot. Zlip zlop zlee.*

(Class giggles)

Mrs. L.:	Everybody running to the coconut tree. That sounds like a rhyme to me! Who has another idea?
Anna:	How about *Drit drat droodle loot*?
Mrs. L.	That's a good one! If I erase our first invented line, we may forget it, so I'll write our new idea underneath the first one.

Bobby: Then put *mlip mlop mlee*.

Sara: That's too hard to say. Keep the *drit drat* but *mlip* is too hard.

Mrs. L.: What do you think, Bobby?

Bobby: Okay, how about *Bip bop bee*?

Students: Better!

Stephanie: I have one. *Flit flat floodle sloot*.

Olivia: Then *Spip spop spee*.

Mrs. L.: I'll write this down. Do you notice how only the beginning sounds change while the *it at oodle oot, ip op ee* stays the same? Any new ideas?

Rachel: This one starts with *p-h* not *f*: *Phit phat phoodle zoot. Quip quop quee*.

Mrs. L.: Great! I think we could do this all day and never come up with the same idea twice. Let's write one more.

Molly: *Nit nat noodle shoot. Mip mop mee*.

Mrs. L.: These are very good rhymes! Let's read our whole list and see if we have any that we like better than the original one.

Class: Skit skat skoodle doot. Flip flop flee.
Blit blat bloodle eoot. Zlip zlop zlee.
Drit drat droodle loot. Bip bop bee.
Flit flat floodle sloot. Spip spop spee.
Phit phat phoodle zoot. Quip quop quee.
Nit nat noodle shoot. Mip mop mee.

Katie: I like the beginning of *Drit drat* best. But I like *Flip flop* best at the end.

Stephanie: We could mix up the parts!

Carrie: I like *Drit drat droodle loot. Flip flop flee*.

Mrs. L.: How about *Blit blat bloodle zoot. Quip quop quee*. Oh, no—now I know we could do this all day. These nonsense words are endless! Isn't it amazing that just by changing a few letters, we've created our own set of words! I think John Archambault and Bill Martin Jr. would be impressed with your invented words. Who knows, maybe some of the ideas you invented are ones they never thought of.

Carrie: Oh, no, if they liked our idea better, they'd have to change the whole book and that's a lot of work!

Mrs. L.: You're right. Maybe we should keep these wonderful nonsense words a secret.

Bobby: Maybe we could pick a line to illustrate on our own?

Mrs. L.: That's a great idea. After you illustrate your new favorite lines, we'll display them in the hallway for others to see.

Carrie: Just don't let the real authors see them!

Having fun with <u>Chicka Chicka Boom Boom</u>

So that is exactly what we did. The next day the students did a little more brainstorming in groups until they each had a favorite new rhyme to illustrate. The ideas for rhyming word sentences were endless and the giggles continuous as the students discovered a few other favorite lines on their own.

A favorite invented line for Chicka Chicka Boom Boom. ▶

Book Celebrations: Activities to Extend Learning

Chicka Chicka Boom Boom on Tape

For more *Chicka Chicka Boom Boom* fun, share the companion audiocassette (Simon & Schuster, 1992), which features several creative rereadings of the story by Ray Charles and another by some very expressive children. On the flip side of the tape, the words are put to music as the children read along. Then author John Archaumbault tells how the idea for *Chicka Chicka Boom Boom* came to be, shares other favorite rhyming poems, and invites children to join in a reversed version of *Chicka Chicka Boom Boom* that goes from *Z* to *A*! Students love listening to this taped version of a favorite book again and again.

More Books With a Beat

Children love reading and rereading books with a beat. Don't be surprised at how hard they will work at finding the beat and how many times they will reread a book to get it just right. Rereading words over and over again is sure to help students expand their vocabulary of words known instantly, not to mention the fact that reading for fun is what makes beginning readers into lifelong readers.

Since it often takes a few readings to find the implied beat, rehearse the books on your own a few times before sharing them with your class. Practicing these books repeatedly and committing them to memory will give you a motivating transition activity—"Let's see if we can clean up the math materials in the time it takes me to recite *Chicka Chicka Boom Boom* by heart." Although there are hundreds of "books with a beat," the four listed below are a few of my favorites for challenging students to play with the rhythm of language.

JAMBERRY BY BRUCE DEGAN: "One berry, two berry, pick me a blueberry. Hatberry, shoeberry in my canoeberry." This classic story is a favorite in many primary classrooms. You'll easily discover the beat and, if you look closely, you'll notice some foreshadowing as several of the upcoming animals visit the page prior to their description in the text. Have a discussion about invented "berry" words and rhyming words or use this book to talk about invented compound words. Have a cooking lesson and make blueberry cobbler; compile favorite blueberry recipes into a class "Jamberry Cookbook"; write stories about summertime adventures. The possibilities for extending learning with this book are endless!

MISS SPIDER'S TEA PARTY BY DAVID KIRK: This counting book is great to use with your less confident readers because it has just one sentence per page with beautiful picture clues. This book does, however, feature some challenging words for more able readers to decode, such as *gasped, silently,* and *refused*. You may need to read this book several times to find the beat. *Miss Spider's Tea Party* is a good book to use to talk about "sound-alike" rhyming words since many of the rhyming pairs are not "look-alike" pairs.

17 KINGS AND 42 ELEPHANTS BY MARGARET MAHY: This book has one of the most interesting beats I have ever read:

> Seventeen kings on forty-two elephants
> Going on a journey through a wild wet night,
> Baggy ears like big umbrellaphants,
> Little eyes a-gleaming in the jungle light. (pages 1–2)

As with any rhyming book, read it several times to find the way all the words fit the beat. Children love to hear *17 Kings and 42 Elephants* read aloud and can't help but tap feet and sway to the rhythm of this book. It's almost as if there are jungle drums playing in the background or elephant feet stampeding down the hallway as you read this book!

PIGS IN THE MUD IN THE MIDDLE OF THE RUD BY LYNN PLOURDE: "Oh no. Won't do. Gotta shoo. But who?" Let your students encounter nonsense rhyming word pairs like *shmuffle* and *shuffle*, a foot-stomping rhythm, words with *-ed* endings, and one feisty grandma in this comical book with a predictable pattern that beginning readers will love.

Sharing a book with a beat for Read Aloud time

> **MANAGEMENT TIP**
>
> Do your best to read a book aloud with your students every day. Allow time to talk about favorite parts, answer questions that arise, and discuss illustrations and the words used to tell the story. This time for discussion is valuable for expanding young readers' appreciation for literature—and also provides a wealth of books to be added to the Favorite Books Box!

More Nonsense

Dr. Seuss was a master of invented words. *There's a Wocket in My Pocket* is just one example of a story that allows students to sound out words using rhyming word clues. I begin this activity by introducing some of Dr. Seuss's friends to my students: "Last night, I sat down on the sofa beside what I thought was my dog, Sydney, but I was sitting next to a Bofa! As I reached to turn on the lamp, I accidentally touched a Zamp!" After reading *There's a Wocket in My Pocket*, we brainstorm other objects with invented rhyming counterparts. Then I give students a chance to write a short story about their own silly invented characters.

> One rainy day, as I was looking out the window, a Zindow appeared out of nowhere. At first I was scared, but he smiled and said, "My friend Shmook would like you to read us a book. And if you don't mind, cook some noodles for the Fluffoodles." I thought I was dreaming, so I gave myself a pinch, and a Troulder patted my shoulder.

Word Power Assessment: True Clues—Rhyming Words

Invented words are a fun and effective way to evaluate your students' understanding of rhyming words. Copy word parts such as those listed below onto colored oak tag and laminate the set for safekeeping. Use cut-out alphabet letters to provide a manipulative-based assessment of rhyming word families. Have students meet with you individually to add consonants, one at a time, to each card and then read the newly invented word. Although true words can be made from the word parts, more nonsense words will be created than real ones. Since you are not assessing students' ability to read word parts but rather their ability to read new words created by adding different beginning letters to word parts, say the word chunks as often as possible, as illustrated below in my assessment of John.

___ittle   ___addy   ___urp   ___effer

___ora   ___onk   ___azzle

John, Grade 1

HELPING A RELUCTANT READER WITH RHYMING WORDS

John is a first grader with a limited sight-word vocabulary. With few words committed to memory, he pauses frequently to sound out many words by their individual sounds and, as a result, his reading fluency and comprehension suffer. John read *Five Little Monkeys Jumping on the Bed* and *Brown Bear, Brown Bear, What Do You See?*, two repetitive rhyming word books, again and again during independent reading time. I decided to use the magic of rhyming words to help John see that knowing how to read just one word would help him read many other words with similar letters. I hoped rhyming words would give John his first strategy for attacking unknown words and boost his reading confidence as well. I arranged some Alphabet Fun Letters on the table in alphabetical order, copied the word parts listed above onto index cards, and was ready to meet with John.

Mrs. L.: I was wondering if you would help me invent some new words using the Alphabet Fun Letters and word parts I have on these cards.

John: I'll try.

Mrs. L.: The first one is *a-z-z-l-e*. Do you know how to say this?

John: No. Maybe it's *izzle*.

Mrs. L.: Very close—it has an *a* sound so these letters spell *azzle*. Would you please add a *b* to the front of *azzle* and tell me what it spells?

John:	*Bizzle.*
Mrs. L.:	Close. Remember, this is *azzle*, not *izzle*.
John:	*Bazzle?*
Mrs. L.:	Right, John! B with *azzle* makes *bazzle*. Let's add a *c* with *azzle*—it will rhyme with *bazzle*.
John:	*Cazzle.*
Mrs. L.:	Right. Now try *d*.
John:	That would be *dazzle*—I've heard of this word before.
Mrs. L.:	"You are dazzling me with your good reading," or "I like your dazzling smile!" *Dazzle* is a word used to describe how amazing something is. Try *f*.
John:	*Fazzle.*
Mrs. L.:	G would be…
John:	*Gazzle.*
Mrs. L.:	H would be….
John:	*Hazzle.*
Mrs. L.:	You are good at this, John. All you have to do is read *azzle* and add a new sound and look at all the other words you can read! That's pretty amazing. Let's try another word part. This next one is u-r-p-*urp*.
John:	Like in *burp*?
Mrs. L.:	Yes. What letter would we add to *urp* to make *burp*?
John:	B.
Mrs. L.:	Right. Go ahead and pick some letters to add to *urp* and tell me what you make.
John:	S would be *sump*.
Mrs. L.:	Close. Remember, these are *urp* words—they'll all rhyme with *burp*.
John:	Oh. Then it would be *burp*, *surp*.
Mrs. L.:	You're doing a nice job with rhyming words, John. I'm glad because knowing about rhyming words can really help you out when you come to a word you're unsure of.
John:	Like *burp* and *surp*?
Mrs. L.:	Or *burp* and *slurp*, or like *bump* and *jump*—I know you can read *jump* which means you can also read *lump*, *dump*, *stump*—
John:	And *wump*!
Mrs. L.:	Yes! And harder words like *trump-et* and *bump-er*. You can read all these words just by knowing how to read three letters when they are put together—u-m-p. Let's try another card.

We continue this pattern of choosing random letters to add to other word parts on the cards. On another day I have John read lists of words such as *at*, *bat*, *cat*, *sat*, *fat*, *mat*, *chat*, and *that* to reinforce his understanding of rhyming words. When reading one-on-one with John, I pause to point out where knowledge about rhyming words can be used to decode an unknown word, further illustrating the application of rhyming words to his real world of reading.

Bleezer's Ice Cream

by Jack Prelutsky

"Bleezer's Ice Cream" from *New Kid on the Block* by Jack Prelutsky. Copyright © 1984 by Jack Prelutsky. Originally published by Greenwillow Books. Used by permission of HarperCollins Publishers.

"Bleezer's Ice Cream" Mini-Book • Cover and Template

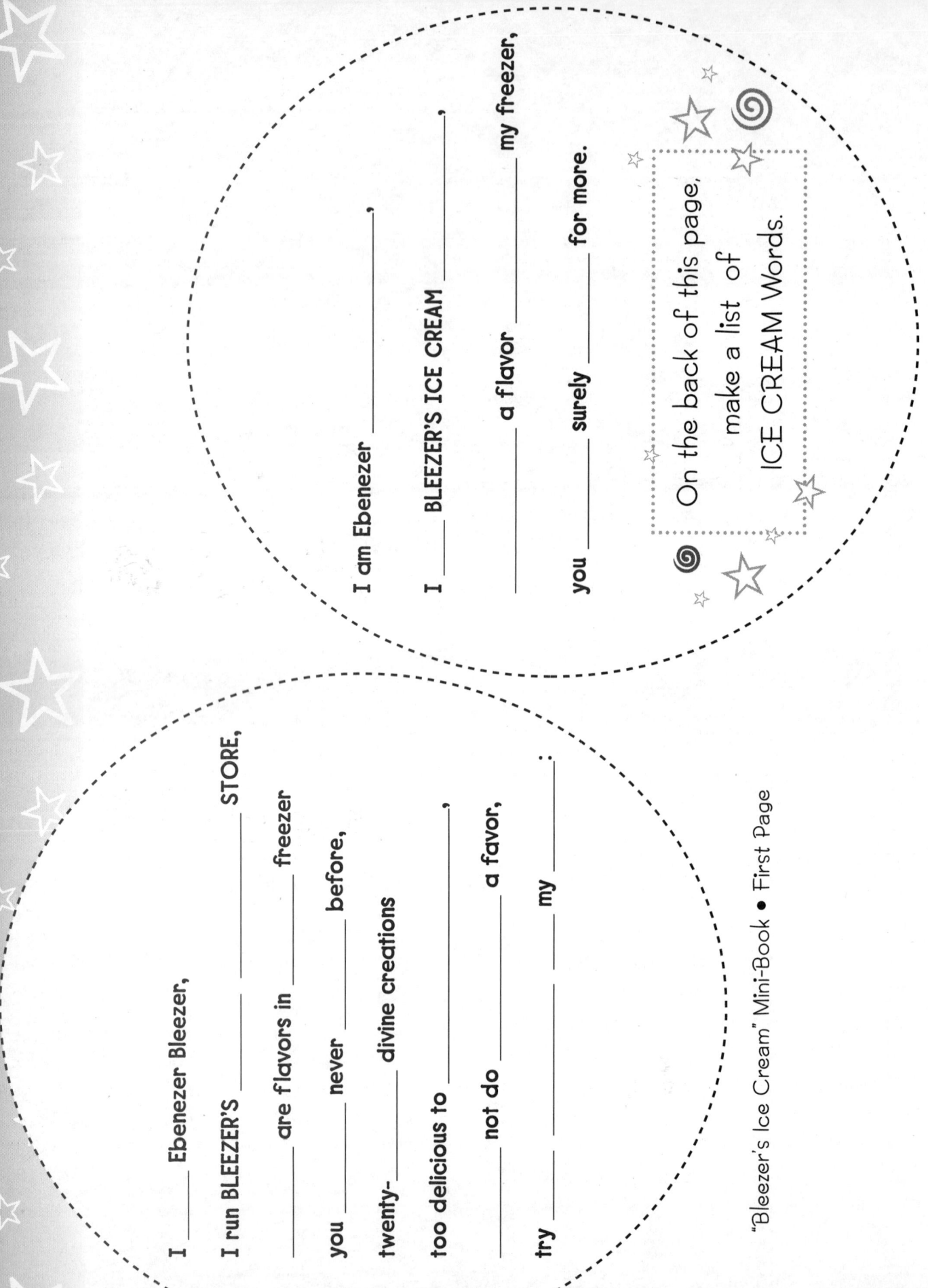

"Bleezer's Ice Cream" Mini-Book • Last Page

I am Ebenezer _____ ,

I _____ BLEEZER'S ICE CREAM _____ my freezer,

_____ a flavor _____ ,

you _____ surely _____ for more.

On the back of this page, make a list of ICE CREAM Words.

"Bleezer's Ice Cream" Mini-Book • First Page

I _____ Ebenezer Bleezer,

I run BLEEZER'S _____ STORE,

_____ are flavors in _____ freezer

you _____ never _____ before,

twenty-_____ divine creations

too delicious to _____ ,

_____ not do _____ a favor,

try _____ my _____ :

Alphabet Fun Letters

A	B	C	D	E
F	G	H	I	J
K	L	M	N	O
P	Q	R	S	T
U	V	W	X	Y
Z	A	E	I	O

Books to Use: Rhyming Words

17 Kings and 42 Elephants by Margaret Mahy (Dial Books for Young Readers, 1987)

Brown Bear, Brown Bear What Do You See? by Bill Martin Jr. (Harcourt Brace & Company, 1967)

Chicka Chicka Boom Boom by Bill Martin Jr. and John Archambault (Simon & Schuster, 1989)

Eating the Alphabet: Fruits and Vegetables From A to Z by Lois Ehlert (Harcourt Brace & Company, 1996)

Feathers for Lunch by Lois Ehlert (Harcourt Brace & Company, 1990)

Fish Eyes: A Book You Can Count On by Lois Ehlert (Harcourt Brace & Company, 1992)

Five Little Monkeys Jumping on the Bed by Eileen Christelow (Clarion Books, 1989)

Jamberry by Bruce Degan (HarperCollins Publishers, 1983)

Miss Spider's Tea Party by David Kirk (Scholastic Press, 1997)

The New Kid on the Block by Jack Prelutsky (Greenwillow Books, 1984)

Nuts to You by Lois Ehlert (Harcourt Brace & Company, 1993)

Pigs in the Mud in the Middle of the Rud by Lynn Plourde (The Blue Sky Press, 1997)

Something Big Has Been Here by Jack Prelutsky (Greenwillow Books, 1990)

There's a Wocket in My Pocket by Dr. Seuss (Random House, Inc., 1974)

Words With Happy Endings

Mini-Lessons

Mouses or Mice?

Working With Words

Laughed, Giggled and Grinned!

Student Goals

To explore plural endings

To investigate words with *–ing* endings

To investigate words with *–ed* endings

Favorite Books to Use

Mouse Mess by Linnea Riley
Five Little Monkeys Jumping on the Bed by Eileen Christelow
Henry and Mudge Take the Big Test by Cynthia Rylant
Good Books, Good Times! by Lee Bennett Hopkins
Julius by Angela Johnson
The Wizard, the Fairy, and the Magic Chicken by Helen Lester

Mouses or Mice?

GOAL To explore plural endings

Helping kids recognize and understand word endings gives them a great decoding strategy. They learn how to break words into smaller, meaningful parts and how to apply rules that change root words when endings are added. Using literature to explore word endings makes the process fun for everyone.

The first time I saw the cover of Mouse Mess by Linnea Riley, I knew it was a book to share with my first and second graders. The bright cover with the playful mouse stepping over cookies, crackers, and other edible things grabbed my attention. When I opened the cover and saw the picture of the mouse, standing on a pile of cookies and stepping into the next page, I knew I had found a new favorite book!

After picture-reading the story, reading and discussing the rhyming words, talking about a mouse's perspective of our human world, and reading it for fun several times, my students and I take an even closer look at the illustrations of the mouse's snacks. I remove the dust jacket (identical to the cover, in case your copy is jacketless), tack it to the white board with sticky tack, and the students meet me for a mini-lesson that explores plural endings.

<u>Mouse Mess</u> by Linnea Riley

Mrs. L.:	Who remembers my favorite mouse book about food?
Allisa:	Mouse Mess!
Mrs. L.:	You know the first time I saw this book, I had a feeling it would become one of our favorites. When we look at Mouse Mess today, we're going to be word explorers looking for words that have a certain ending. Here's a hint: This ending tells readers that there is more than one of something.
Katie:	Like more than one cookie for the mouse.
Mrs. L.:	Exactly! Pretend you ate all of these (I point to the chocolate cookies on the cover). What did you eat?
Class:	Cookies.
Mrs. L.:	You just said the ending I'm talking about.
Abbey:	Cookie-ssss.
Mrs. L.:	Right. How many cookies? Look closely so that you don't miss any—there are some hidden in the mouse's mess.

Anna: Eleven and a half cookies.

Olivia: That's what I got.

Mrs. L.: Me, too. So are 11 and a half cookies more than one cookie?

Bobby: Yes, ten and a half more than one.

Mrs. L.: Excellent.

Sara: It wouldn't sound right if you said, "He had a mess of 11 cookie." You need an s.

Mrs. L.: I agree. How about if I make a list of all the things that make up a mouse mess. Look for things on the cover in groups of more than one and I'll write these words on the board.

Stephanie: I see pretzels—seven pretzels.

Rachel: There are a bunch of olives, but I don't like olives.

Mrs. L.: I'll write *pretzels* and *olives* on our list under cookies.

Tommy: Don't forget *crackers*.

Anna: And *pickles*.

Matthew: Is that cereal the mouse is stepping on by the cookies?

Sara: Yes, but you don't say *cereals*, so what is it?

Carrie: No, it's corn flakes. Remember the dedication is to her "dad who likes corn flakes," and the box of corn flakes is in the picture.

Mrs. L.: Great remembering! I'll write *corn flakes* under crackers.

Allisa: Cheese.

Mrs. L.: Slices or wedges?

Allisa: Both.

Matthew: Oranges and apples.

Marc: Slices of bread are in the mess—two slices.

Allisa: Jars of mustard and ketchup.

Mrs. L.: Good detecting! I'll add these to our list. Let's read what we have so far:

Class: Cookies, pretzels, olives, crackers, pickles, corn flakes, apples, cheese slices, cheese wedges, oranges, apples, bread slices, jars.

Mrs. L.: Any other things in the mouse mess?

Marc: Maybe we should look inside the book at the picture.

John: Or the words. The words might have s.

Mrs. L.: Good idea. How about if I read the story, and you make sure we haven't missed any words that mean more than one. You've done an excellent job of getting all of the pictures that we see on the cover. Now listen for words that mean more than one as I read the words of the story. Say *stop* whenever you hear a word that means more than one.

> Hush, hush, a little mouse
> is sound asleep inside his house.
> On the stairs, the sound of feet.

Carrie: Stop. *Stairs*.

Mrs. L.: Great. I'll add this to our list. Mouse didn't hear the sound of feet on a *stair*; he heard it on the *stairs*.

Carrie: Stairs are not part of the mouse mess, but they mean more than one.

Mrs. L.: You're right. Let's include all the words that mean more than one, whether they're part of the mess or not. There's another word on this page that means more than one, but it doesn't end in *s*. The word changes when you have more than one. You have two of them.

Sara: Feet!

Mrs. L.: Right.

Katie: There's no such thing as *feets*. But one of them is a *foot*.

Mrs. L.: Exactly! I'll keep reading.

> Mouse is up. It's time to eat!

Tommy: Stop. *It's* ends in *s*.

Mrs. L.: Yes, it does. Let's think about the word *it's*. Does *it's* mean more than one?

Marc: No. You can't have more than one *it*.

Sara: Besides, *it's* means *it is*.

Mrs. L.: Right. Sometimes words end in *s* simply because it's the last letter of the word. I'll read the next page.

> Crunch-crunch, he wants a cracker.
> Crunch-munch, a cookie snacker.

You didn't stop me for *wants*—any reason?

Anna: It doesn't mean more than one.

Mrs. L.: What great word detectives you are! I'll keep reading:

> Crackle-sweep, he rakes corn flakes
> and jumps into the pile he makes.

Chris: We already said *corn flakes*.

Molly: But we don't have *rakes*.

Olivia: Or *jumps*.

David: I don't think they are more-than-one words.

Mrs. L.: Think about the meaning of the words *he rakes corn flakes*.

Carrie: Mouse only has one rake in the picture. It's a fork.

Mrs. L.: You're right. You can have more than one rake, but in this sentence *rakes* tells what he is doing, so it's not a word that means more than one; it's an action word.

Bobby: *Jumps* tells what he is doing, too, so don't add it to our list.

Mrs. L.: Good detecting. I'll keep reading.

(We reject *makes*, *spills*, and *falls*; we add *walls* and *tops* to our list. Then we pause to discuss the next sentence when a disagreement arises.)

Mrs. L.:
> Mouse steps back.
> He looks around.

Billy: Steps are like stairs, and we counted *stairs* as an ending that means more than one. We're not talking about one step—it's steps.

Mrs. L.: Let me read the sentence again, and you tell me what you think:

> Mouse steps back.

Matthew: See, we're not talking about steps like stairs. We're talking about stepping with your feet.

Mrs. L.: So steps is an action word in this sentence.

Class: Yes!

Mrs. L.: Let's continue; we're almost finished.

> He can't believe the mess he's found.
> "Who made this awful mess?" asks Mouse.
> "These people need to clean their house!"

Mrs. L.: You didn't stop me.

Bobby: There's no s word.

Mrs. L.: But there is a word that means more than one: "These people need to—"

Molly: Oh, *people!* Not one person needs to clean it, people do—more than one person.

Mrs. L.: Good detecting. Let's continue.

> Now that mouse is clean and fed,
> he leaves the mess and goes …to bed!

Did we miss any plural endings?

Tommy: Any what?

Mrs. L.: I used a fancy word, didn't I? A *plural ending* is the name for the s on the end of a word when it means more than one. Let's read all the words we found in the book that mean more than one, that have plural endings.

Class: Cookies, pretzels, olives, crackers, pickles, corn flakes, apples, cheese slices, cheese wedges, oranges, apples, bread slices, jars, stairs, feet, walls, tops, people, toes.

Mrs. L.: It sure took a lot of plural endings to make a mouse mess, didn't it! How about if I label our list "Mouse Messes" because I think this mouse enjoys making messes. Please help me spell *messes*.

Matthew: Just add an s. The cover has m-e-s-s. Just add another s: m-e-s-s-s.

Mrs. L.: Wait a minute. That would spell "messs." When I say *messes* there's an extra sound.

Carrie: Is it e-s?

Mrs. L.: Yes, it is. Some words—those that end in s already, for example—need an *e* with the s to show more than one. Some words, like *book*, just have an s. But *mess-es* has e-s.

Anna: So does dresses because it rhymes with *messes*.

Mrs. L.: Excellent! So when you are writing a word and showing that it means more than one, you have to listen closely to the ending sound of the word. Sometimes you add -s and sometimes you add -es.

If you look closely when you're reading, you will notice other words that include -s or -es and there are others that end in -s but don't mean more than one. Still other words, like *people*, change completely to show more than one of a certain thing. Word detectives keep their eyes open for word clues and make new discoveries about words with every page they read.

On another day, I divide the class into groups and give each group a few books from the Favorite Books Box and a copy of More Mouse Messes (page 63). Students are asked to browse through these books to find additional items that could make up a mouse mess. These are classified into single items (such as one orange) or plural items (such as many crackers) that make up a mouse mess and then illustrated on the recording sheet.

Working in "Mouse Mess" groups

A "Mouse Mess" ▶

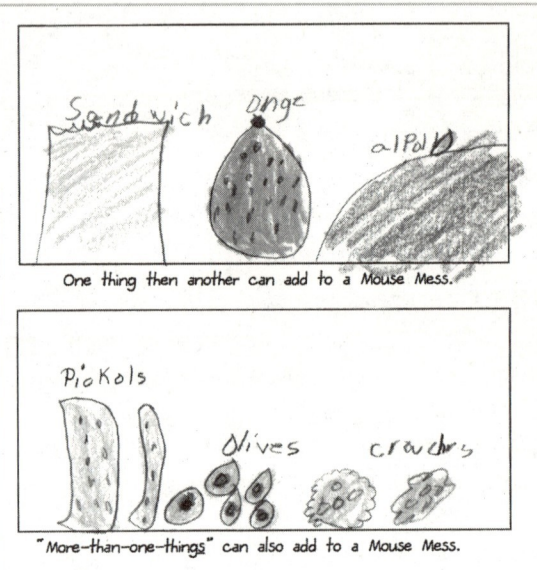

After this independent work time, we gather together to chart some plural rules and an example of each rule:

Plural Rules

- If a word ends in s, add -es to make it plural. (dresses)
- If a word ends in x, add -es to make it plural. (foxes)
- If a word ends in e, just add -s to make it plural (noses)
- If a word ends in y, the y changes to i and you add -es.
- Some words stay the same when they are plural. (deer, fish)
- Some words change completely whenever they are plural (foot—feet, child—children, person—people, mouse—mice)

Note: Some words that end in s are action words. (Mouse steps back)

As new discoveries in words are made during Read Aloud or independent reading times, we add these findings to our rules chart. We continue to play with words to better understand the way words work.

Book Celebrations: Activities to Extend Learning

Changing 'Y' to 'I': Using Finger Pencils to Teach Plurals

An important plural rule that requires some practice is:

When a word ends in y, *the* y *changes to* i *before you add* -es.

After reading *Blueberries for Sal* by Robert McCloskey, we discuss how difficult it would be to make a blueberry pie with just one blueberry or eat just one blueberry, and how disappointing it would be to go berry picking and find only one blueberry. I write *We love blueberrys* on the board and say, "This doesn't look right," before explaining the change that occurs in words that end in the letter *y*. I chant "*y* changes to *i* before you add *e-s*" and invite the students to repeat the rule with me. On the board, I cross out the *y*, write *i* above the crossed out *y*, and add *-es* to the end of the word. While I write it on the board, the children copy the changes on a friend's back using "finger pencils."

blueberr~~y~~ i + -es = blueberries

We do the same for *strawberry, blackberry, cherry, kitty,* and any other word ending in *y* that the children think of. Each time I write a word on the board, I invite the students to copy the word in a different way—in the air, on the floor, on their legs. We overdramatize the erasing of *y* to help commit this procedure to memory. I explain that with practice, erasers are not worn down as quickly, and they will soon automatically change *y* to *i* before adding *-es*.

Practicing plurals with finger pencils ▶

If You Give a Mouse a Cookie: More Practice With Plurals

Here's another mouse book that, with a little creativity, can be used to practice plural endings. Changing the title of *If You Give a Mouse a Cookie* (Numeroff, 1985) to *If You Give Two Mice Two Cookies* will allow you and your students to rewrite a favorite circle story while reinforcing plural endings and handwriting skills. Students will quickly see that the original words *a cookie* become *two cookies,* and other words also change when they become plural (for example, *he* and *she* become *they*).

Pass out lined writing paper with space for an illustration on which students copy two sentences a day for handwriting practice. Begin by writing the original sentence followed by the invented sentence on the board for students to copy. Have them underline plural endings and double-underline other words with plural meanings.

If you give a mouse a cookie, he's going to ask for a glass of milk.

If you give two mice two cookies, they're going to ask for two glasses of milk.

Over the next several days, have students select sentences to rewrite independently or with partners. After a few productive days of handwriting and plural word practice, add a construction-paper cover to collected samples. Students then have booklets to take home to share with their families. Don't forget to share *If You Give a Pig a Pancake* (1998) and *If You Give a Moose a Muffin* (1991), also by Laura Joffe Numeroff, for more read-aloud giggles.

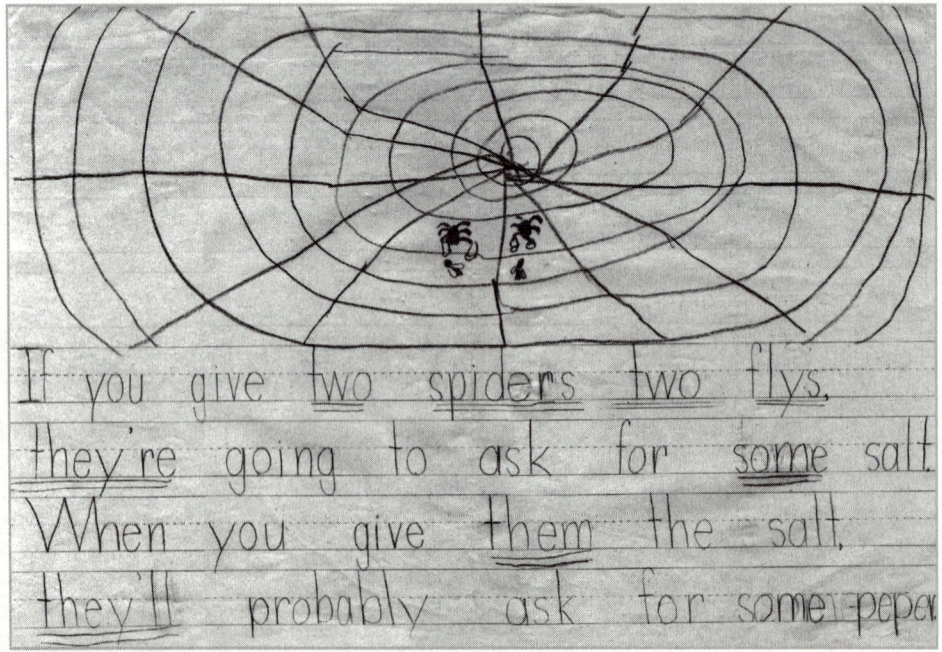

Practice writing plurals

Good Books, Good Times! Good Words, Good Rhymes!

Chart the cover poem found on page 17 of Lee Bennett Hopkins's book of selected poems *Good Books, Good Times!* (HarperCollins, 1990) for a list of 16 plural words from *friends* to *adventures*. After a good time sharing these good things, have your students add their own good ideas to this list, using plural words that rhyme.

> Good pets.
> Good walks.
> Good snacks.
> Good talks.

Working With Words

GOAL To investigate words with *-ing* endings

Five Little Monkeys Jumping on the Bed adds playfulness to a lesson on the -ing ending: We generate our own escapades for these monkeys using words with -ing endings. Throughout our discussion of -ing, I alternate between saying -ing and spelling i-n-g, which reinforces both the spelling and sound of this ending. After our lesson, -ing is committed to memory by nearly all of the students. I also try to emphasize any words that I use while explaining -ing, and the students catch on to the importance and frequency of this ending in our language. We discuss the need to add a double consonant in consonant-vowel-consonant words like running and to drop the silent e before adding -ing in words like making. The rules for using -ing are popular with beginning readers, who like knowing all the clues up front.

A well-loved book from my classroom: <u>Five Little Monkeys Jumping on the Bed</u> *by Eileen Christelow* ▶

Mrs. L.:	Yesterday for Read Aloud I read the book *Five Little Monkeys Jumping on the Bed* by Eileen Christelow. I can't get the story out of my head. "The mama called the doctor. The doctor said..."
Class:	"No more monkeys jumping on the bed!"
Mrs. L.:	It has a great beat, doesn't it? You know Eileen Christelow has another book about the five little monkeys' escapades.
Sara:	*Five Little Monkeys Sitting in a Tree.*
Mrs. L.:	Right! There is an endless number of adventures that Eileen Christelow could write about—five little monkeys could be doing so many different things.
Tommy:	Like playing soccer.

John: Eating spaghetti.

Greg: Or watching TV.

Mrs. L.: Those could be silly stories! Today I want to think about other possible titles that would work on the cover of this book about monkeys. Let's keep the *Five Little Monkeys*—I'll write this on the board. Now look at the cover for ideas that describe what the five little monkeys are doing.

Marc: What about *Five Little Monkeys Wearing Pajamas*?

Mrs. L.: That works. I'll write *Wearing Pajamas* under *Five Little Monkeys*. They are wearing pajamas, aren't they?

Alex: How about *Laughing on the Bed*?

Mrs. L.: Sure. I'll write *Laughing* under *Wearing Pajamas* and keep adding your ideas to this list.

Olivia: Like *Grinning on the Bed*.

Allisa: Or *Smiling on the Bed*.

Mrs. L.: You are good at this!

David: *Dancing on the Bed*.

Mrs. L.: I can hardly write your ideas fast enough. Do you notice anything the same about all of these words?

Matthew: The last three letters—i-n-g.

Mrs. L.: Right. I wonder why *-ing* is on the end of all these words. Let's read these i-n-g words.

Class: *Wearing, laughing, grinning, smiling, dancing.*

Bobby: Oh, I get it. These are all things the monkeys are doing.

Mrs. L.: So they are action words, right?

Class: Yes.

Mrs. L.: Are you wearing pajamas right now?

Class: No!

Mrs. L.: But you are thinking right now, aren't you? And some of you are giggling. What you're doing right now is described with an *-ing* ending. *Sitting, thinking, learning*— *-ing* makes a word a working word, the thing or things you are doing. Can you think of any other working words to describe what the monkeys are doing?

Greg: They're *partying* on the bed.

Marc: Or *twisting* on the bed.

Cassie: *Bouncing* on the bed.

Mrs. L.: These are wonderful ideas. Now, let's take the *i-n-g* ending off of these words to find the root words, or the words that can stand alone.

Billy: *Wearing* has the root word *wear*.

Mrs. L.: Great. I'll underline this part: w-e-a-r.

Stephanie: *Laughing* is *laugh*.

Mrs. L.: Super.

Abbey: *Grinning* is *grin*.

Mrs. L.: Would you spell that please?

Abbey:	G-r-i-n-n.
Sara:	That doesn't look right.
Mrs. L.:	I agree. If I underline g-r-i-n-n, that leaves i-n-g. But this is a kind of word that can trick you.
Bobby:	You must have added an extra n by mistake.
Mrs. L.:	Actually, I added the extra n on purpose! Some words need an extra ending letter added to them before you add the i-n-g.
Matthew:	How do you know if they need the letter?
Mrs. L.:	Lots of practice is the best way to learn. When you are reading a book, always be a word detective and try to examine words closely. Now you can look for words that end in i-n-g. This will help you do what Sara did a minute ago. She said, "That doesn't look right" when she saw g-r-i-n-n by itself. Trust yourself—if you think a word looks funny when you write it down, explore a little further, look for the book-spelling of the word.
Bobby:	Like in a dictionary.
Mrs. L.:	Chances are, your mind is giving you a hint.
Tommy:	It's hard to know when something is spelled the right way.
Mrs. L:	I agree, but the more you read, the better your eyes and mind will be at helping you write words correctly on your own. There are some rules to follow that will help you as well. We'll talk about those on another day. Right now, let's continue to find more root words and see if we discover anything else. What's the next word on our list?
Greg:	Smiling.
Mrs. L:	What is the root word?
Alex:	Smile.
Mrs. L:	Right. Spell it, please.
Class:	S-m-i-l.
Marc:	E! Smile ends with e. I know it does.
Sara:	Yes, he's right, it does.
Mrs. L.:	You've just discovered a root word rule. When a word ends in silent e, you drop the e before adding -ing. Dancing is the same kind of word. If I remove the -ing, I'm left with d-a-n-c. But dance is spelled d-a-n-c-e. The e falls off before you add i-n-g.
Billy:	D-a-n-c-e-i-n-g would look funny.
Mrs. L.:	I'll write it on the board.
Tommy:	That's not right. You need to erase the e before the -ing.
Mrs. L.:	See, your eyes and mind are already working together to discover what looks right and what doesn't. That tells me you've read many books and are becoming excellent word detectives. What's the next -ing word on our list?

(We continue down our list, examining root words and discussing root word rules. To end the lesson, we reread our list of -ing words together. Kids now have a good sense of how the -ing form of a word is made; they also have a new word power strategy for decoding words that end in -ing.)

Book Celebrations: Activities to Extend Learning

More Monkey Business

The next day, at the students' suggestion, we make a list of actions the five little monkeys could be doing instead of jumping on the bed. Eating pizza in a tree, picking bananas off a tree, reading books at the library, playing at the park, and chasing butterflies in the yard were just a few suggestions made by my "21 little students."

After brainstorming a few ideas, students illustrate a jacket cover for a favorite invented title for a new five little monkeys' book. During sharing time, we discuss the root word of the *-ing* word in each new title. This allows us to further discuss changes that may be needed before adding *-ing*, and the students' prowess as word detectives continues to improve!

Designing book jackets

"Five Little Monkeys Laughing on the Bed" ▶

Rules to Read by: Consonant-Vowel-Consonant Words

After a brief lesson that refreshes the students' memories about which letters are vowels and which letters are consonants, we discuss a rule that was mentioned during our mini-lesson on *-ing* endings. I show how a simple word like *sit* is a consonant-vowel-consonant word: *s* is a consonant, *i* is a vowel, and *t* is another consonant. I explain that when *sit* becomes *sitting*, a second *t* must be added before the *-ing* ending because this is the rule that consonant-vowel-consonant words usually follow. We do the same for *bat, run,* and *nap.*

Next, we move on to words with an initial consonant blend, such as *grin.* I explain that blends like *gr* count as one beginning consonant since the sounds of *g* and *r* are blended together. That's why the *n* in *grinning* must be doubled before adding *-ing.* We try a few more words, like *spin, kid, beg,* and *trot,* exploring the c-v-c structure and doubling the consonant before adding *-ing.*

Mama Call<u>ed</u> the Doctor: Writing Stories With <u>-ed</u> Endings

Invite the five little monkeys to a mini-lesson on words with the *-ed* ending. Ask students to think of what else might happen to the five little monkeys—perhaps they climbed a tree and one fell down and skinned a knee, or tripped on a hose and scraped a nose, for example. In this fun writing lesson, students write about a new monkey mishap which causes Mama to call the doctor for each of the five little monkeys. Compile these student stories into a classroom anthology called *Monkey Adventure Stories.*

One story begins: "Five Little Monkeys jumping on the trampoline. One landed in outer space..." ▶

Laughed, Giggled, and Grinned!

MINI-LESSON 6

GOAL To investigate words with *-ed* endings

The day before I taught the following mini-lesson for the first time, I had been reading Henry and Mudge Take the Big Test by Cynthia Rylant. It struck me that Cynthia Rylant used many words with *-ed* endings to tell of Mudge's dog-school experience. With further examination of the first short story, I realized that there were 22 words with this ending on just 15 pages of brief text. So I decided "The Smart Dog" would be a perfect story for examining words with *-ed* endings. Keep in mind that any short story or book set in the past could work with this lesson.

A mini-lesson that focuses on *-ed* endings is helpful for broadening students' understanding of words that show something has already happened—the past tense. Students quickly discover similarities between *-ed* and other endings: double consonants are needed in consonant-vowel-consonant words; some words (like run) change completely when used in the past tense (ran); and silent e words only need a d added to show past tense.

When spoken, the *-ed* ending is added to words automatically by beginning readers. But when written, young children, using phonetic spelling, often eliminate the e and simply write a d or in some instances a t. The different rules for using *-ed* make this a skill well worth exploring with beginning word detectives.

To begin this lesson, I give each child a lap-sized chalkboard or white board to use for recording. As I reread the first story of Henry and Mudge Take the Big Test, called "The Smart Dog," the students listen for words that end in *-ed*.

Henry and Mudge Take the Big Test by Cynthia Rylant ▶

Mrs. L.: I was reading one of our favorite books yesterday, and I noticed that the author uses lots of words with a particular ending. Here's a hint about this ending: You used this ending at recess this morning if you played on the monkey bars, jumped rope, or kicked a soccer ball.

Olivia: Words that end in *d*?

53

Mrs. L.: You've thought of half of the ending. There's a letter before the *d*, although you really *don't* hear this letter. If this letter made a sound in the word, it would be *played*.

Carrie: Is it *e-d*?

Mrs. L.: Yes, it is. This ending—*-ed*—changes the meaning of a word in a certain way. If you say, "I will play soccer," that means one thing. But if you say, "I played soccer," it means something else.

Allisa: If you *played* soccer it means you did it.

Sara: You already did it.

Mrs. L.: Exactly. The *-ed* ending is added to words to show something was done in the past. I *jumped* rope at recess this morning. I *kicked* a ball and made a goal. When you talk, you automatically put *-ed* on the end of your spoken words. But when you read or write words that need this *-ed* ending, you have to pay attention. If you don't put *-ed* on a word, the meaning is changed.

Bobby: But when you say *-ed* on the end of a word, you only say the *d*.

Mrs. L.: Right. Lots of times, the *e* doesn't even make a sound, but it is still part of the ending.

I'd like to reread the first story in *Henry and Mudge Take the Big Test*. As you listen to this story called "The Smart Dog," I'd like you to count on your fingers each *-ed* word you hear on a page. After I finish each page, hold up fingers to show me how many *-ed* words you heard. Then together we'll write these *-ed* words on the white board.

Chris: Don't read too fast.

Mrs. L.: I'll stop after each page and give you time to copy the *-ed* words we discover. When you're ready for me to go to the next page, you can give me a smile so that I know to continue reading.

Alex: How many *-ed* words will we find?

Mrs. L.: There are 22 *-ed* words in the story. Let's see if we can find them all. Here's page one:

> On a sunny day Henry and Henry's mother and Henry's big dog Mudge were sitting on their front porch. A man with a collie walked by.

Mrs. L.: Most of you are holding up one finger. What is the *-ed* word?

John: Walked.

Mrs. L.: Great. I'll write this on the board with the *-ed* ending in red. I'll read the next page.

> Suddenly the man stopped. "Sit," said the man. The collie sat. "Down," said the man. The collie lay down.

Anna: The word was *stopped*.

Mrs. L.: Here's *stopped* on page six. I'll walk around so you can see how Cynthia Rylant spelled it. I'll write *s-t-o-p-p* then *-ed* in red.

Carrie: No. *Stop* is spelled *s-t-o-p*.

Mrs. L.: Why do you think there are two *p*'s in this word?

Greg: Maybe Cynthia Rylant misspelled it.

Mrs. L.: No, it's spelled correctly. Think about what you already know about adding *-ing* to words that have a consonant-vowel-consonant pattern.

Billy: Oh! I get it. You must have to double the *p* before adding *-ed*.

Carrie: I think you would double *p* before adding *-ing* to stop.

Mrs. L.: Great word detecting! *St* is a consonant blend, *o* is a vowel, and *p* is another consonant. C-v-c works the same for *-ed* words. So I'll write this special doubled *p* in blue and the *-ed* in red. Page seven is next.

> Henry looked at Mudge. Mudge looked at Henry. They both looked at the collie.

Mrs. L.: Three words?

David: *Looked* is the word, all three times.

Mrs. L.: Since this word repeats, let's write *looked* with three tallies.

Looked |||

We're on page eight now.

> "Stay," said the man. Then he walked a long way down the street. He didn't look back. The collie stayed. The man turned down another street and disappeared. The collie stayed.

Mrs. L.: Some of you are holding up three fingers, others four, and there are even a few showing five fingers. How about if I reread this page more slowly. You put up a finger to keep track of each word you hear. I'll do the same.

(I reread page eight, counting each word with an *-ed* ending.)

Mrs. L.: 1, 2, 3, 4, 5.

Alex: *Walked* was the first word. Put another tally next to *walked*.

Mrs. L.: The next words after "walked a long way down the street" are "He didn't look back. The collie stayed."

Cassie: S-t-a-y and then *-ed*.

Mrs. L.: "The man turned" is next.

Abbey: T-e-r-n then *-ed*.

Marc: No, t-u-r-n then *-ed*.

Mrs. L.: U is right. There are two more *-ed* words on this page.

Tommy: *Disappeared* is one.

David: And *stayed* again.

Mrs. L.: I'll put another tally next to *stayed*. And I'll write *disappeared*.

(I continue reading, discussing, and recording words with *-ed* endings.)

Chris: Finally, they *smiled*.

Mrs. L.: This is a tricky word. I'll write *s-m-i-l* then *-ed*. But the root word of *smile* has an *e* at the end as part of the word.

Bobby: Maybe there are two *e*'s.

Mrs. L.:	Actually, since *smile* already ends in *e*, I don't need to put another *e*; I just add a *d*. So I'll write the *e* in black, then trace over it in red since this *e* really has two jobs in this word. Last page.

(We complete the story and our recording of *-ed* words.)

Mrs. L.:	Excellent word detecting! I would say you are becoming experts on *-ed* endings.
Rachel:	They're pretty easy.
Mrs. L.:	Remembering to write them should be easier to do with practice too. As with everything we learn about reading and writing, it seems there are some words that just don't fit what we know. In fact, in the story I just read, there are a few more words that mean something already happened or was done in the past, but these words don't have *-ed* on the end of them.
Bobby:	No, I'm pretty sure we found all the words.
Mrs. L.:	Yes, you did find all the words that ended in *-ed*. Remember when we were talking about *-s* and *-es* endings we noticed that some words change completely to show more than one—*child* becomes *children* and *mouse* becomes *mice*.
Matthew:	Plural words.
Mrs. L.:	Right. Well, there are some words that change completely to show that something already happened. In a few minutes, we are going to go eat lunch.
Jonathan:	Good, I'm hungry.
Mrs. L.:	Well, when you get back from lunch you will have already eaten lunch. Will you say, "We eated our lunch?"
Class:	No! We ate our lunch.
Mrs. L.:	Exactly. The word *eat* becomes *ate*, not *eated*, to show that this action was done sometime in the past. There are other words like this too. The good thing is that when you read, say, or even write these words, your mind will tell you what word to use because it just makes sense one certain way—like when to use the words *eat* or *ate*.

When you were first learning how to talk, you may have said these words incorrectly. You had to learn by listening to others talk that *-ed* was added to certain words. You just had to practice in order to learn which words needed *-ed* and which words didn't. Now you have to pay attention to make sense of what you are reading. If something doesn't make sense, you need to reread it until it makes sense. Sometimes this means making sure you included an *-ed* on the end of a word. It's also good to understand words because the more details you know about words—like their endings—the easier it is to attack a word you don't know. Now, when you read a word with *-ed*, cover up the *-ed* to make the word look smaller for sounding out.

During silent reading, let's keep our eyes open for words that show something happened in the past. Look closely to see if these words have *-ed* or if the word changes completely. You may be surprised at some of the other words you discover that mean something happened in the past. |

Book Celebrations: Activities to Extend Learning

Endings at a Glance

To show students how some root words stay the same before *-ed* is added and others change completely, I begin a chart of the words we discuss as a group. We spend one lesson brainstorming action words, or verbs, then add *-ed* to show these actions in the past tense. The chart hangs in the classroom as a visual aid for future reference during independent writing times.

Another story to try for root words that change is "School" from *Henry and Mudge Take the Big Test*. Some of the words used in the past tense are *bought, thought, drove,* and *told*.

Root Words That Stay the Same When -ed Is Added:		Root Words That Change When -ed Is Added:	
root	-ed	root	-ed
drool	drooled	say	said
snore	snored	see	saw
smile	smiled	eat	ate
frown	frowned	read	read (only the pronunciation is changed)
start	started		
roll	rolled	teach	taught
disappear	disappeared	sit	sat
turn	turned	write	wrote
stay	stayed	swim	swam
walk	walked	run	ran
talk	talked	sing	sang
look	looked	tell	told

Pet Pictures: What Can Smart Pets Do?

Mudge drooled and rolled very well! What else can a smart pet do? Using copies of page 64, ask students to think of four smart things a pet they know has done. They should draw and label four pictures depicting these things smart pets can do. My smart dogs have *chased*, *whined*, *begged*, and *barked*. Kids don't need to know Mudge's story to enjoy this activity.

◀ Sara's smart pets

Synonym Challenge

Expand your students' vocabulary while practicing *-ed* endings. Challenge students to think of synonyms for the *-ed* words in "The Smart Dog" or any favorite story. After thinking of synonyms, reread the story with the new *-ed* words:

Smart Dog Word	Synonym
walked	strolled
stopped	ceased
looked	spied
stayed	paused
disappeared	vanished
rolled	spiraled
started	began
frowned	pouted
smiled	grinned
snored	??????
drooled	slobbered

Skip the -ed

Try reading a story eliminating the appropriate *-ed* endings and see how long it takes your students to notice! Once they've discovered your game, invite students to stop you as you continue to skip the *-ed*. Students can signal an incorrectly read word by clapping this hands, snapping a finger, or waving a small handmade paper stop sign. This game sharpens listening skills while giving students practice at using endings appropriately.

Some good choices for books with *-ed* endings on nearly every page are *Julius* by Angela Johnson (1993), *Sylvester and the Magic Pebble* by William Steig (1969), and *Monster Mama* by Liz Rosenberg (1993).

Have students take a few minutes to make a paper stop sign attached to a popsicle stick. Keep the stop signs together in an easily accessible place so you can quickly pass them out for word power review lessons in which students listen and stop you when they hear a particular kind of special word.

Student-made stop signs come in handy for word power mini-lessons.

The Wizard the Fairy and the Magic Chicken

On another day, use *The Wizard the Fairy and the Magic Chicken* by Helen Lester (1983) to list lots of *-ed* words that can be used in place of *said*. As the fairy, the wizard and the magic chicken continue to outdo each other with their amazing powers, the words used in their conversation illustrate the characters' escalating feelings. The three *bellowed, screeched, yelled,* and *glared,* and then agreed about the problem of the story before they *shouted, gasped, puffed,* and *cried* before finally deciding to work together. After chanting, "One, two, three, GO," they cheered their victory over the monsters.

Have students copy this list of synonyms for *said* in a student thesaurus for a handy reference during independent writing time (see page 86 of *Literature-Based Mini-Lessons to Teach Writing* by Susan Lunsford, Scholastic Professional Books, 1998).

Fill in the Endings

To assess students' understanding of word endings, I distribute copies of page 65 and have students fill in *-ing* and *-ed* endings. On this page, students must add the appropriate endings to words in isolation and to words within the context of sentences from our favorite books. Prior to this assessment activity, we review our charts of words with endings and review all the special changes some words must go through, such as doubling a consonant before adding an ending, dropping silent *e* before adding another, or changing completely (for example, *swim* changes to *swam*).

Word Power Assessment: Happy Endings

Pick up any favorite book, use copies of page 66, and you can assess your word detectives in ten minutes. Just read a few simple sentences containing a word with an ending and ask students to record the word on the Happy Endings recording sheet. Or provide copies of page 66 near the Favorite Books Box and students can work independently at classifying and recording words with endings found in selected books.

Anna, Grade 2

HELPING A CAPABLE READER BECOME MORE CAREFUL

Anna is a second grader who reads nearly any word placed in front of her with ease. When reading aloud to me during independent reading time one day, I noticed she was skipping the endings on words without pausing to correct her errors. This led me to believe she was not taking the time to understand what she was reading. But when I asked Anna to read a page of a book to herself and tell me about what she had read, she did so without difficulty. Apparently, Anna was still able to comprehend what she was reading; the endings made only subtle differences in meaning. When reading aloud to others, however, these missed endings hurt the flow of the story, making it difficult for the audience to understand all that she shared.

Since Anna is a very capable reader, I wanted her to slow down and be more careful with her reading. I decided to have Anna take a closer look—and listen—to some sentences with *-ed, -ing, -s,* and *-es* words. I read sentences from a few favorite books, omitting the appropriate endings, to help increase Anna's awareness of sentences that just don't make sense without certain endings.

Mrs. L.: I'd like to read some sentences from a few favorite books while you listen for some words with endings, or should I say, "words that are missing their endings."

Anna: You mean you're going to try and trick me?

Mrs. L.: Not trick you but make you think and listen carefully for sentences that don't make sense.

Anna: I'm ready.

Mrs. L.: Here's a sentence from *Mrs. Katz and Tush* by Patricia Polacco:
When they got home, they call and call for Tush, but she didn't come.

Anna: Call doesn't sound right.

Mrs. L.:	What ending would make this sentence sound better? -ing, -ed, -s, or -es?
Anna:	They probably called and called for Tush—e-d.
Mrs. L.:	I'll point to the sentence in the book. What letters are on the end of call?
Anna:	I was right—e-d.
Mrs. L.:	Great. Please read this sentence with the correct words.
Anna:	"When they got home, they called and called for Tush, but she didn't come."
Mrs. L.:	That sentence needs -ed for it to make sense. I'm glad you listened carefully to what you were reading to include all the appropriate endings. Here's a sentence from *The Paper Bag Princess* by Robert Munsch: I love to eat princess, but I have already eaten a whole castle today.
Anna:	*Princess* should be *princesses*. The dragon likes to eat more than one princess.
Mrs. L.:	What should be added to *princess*?
Anna:	-es.
Mrs. L.:	Excellent. Here's the sentence in the book. Please read this sentence with the appropriate ending.
Anna:	"I love to eat princesses, but I have already eaten a whole castle today." This is fun and you haven't tricked me yet. Find a hard one!
Mrs. L.:	Okay, here's one from *Arthur's Thanksgiving* by Marc Brown: In fact, the principal left the office, laugh.
Anna:	That doesn't make sense. *Lefted* isn't a word, I know. There's only one principal… *laugh* must need an ending. The principal was laughing, I bet.
Mrs. L.:	I guess there's just no tricking you, Anna. It's important to put the endings on words when you read to yourself or out loud so that what you read makes sense.
Anna:	What's the use in reading words if they don't make sense?
Mrs. L.:	Exactly! Understanding what you read is the most important part of being a good reader. Would you like to try a few more?
Anna:	Sure!

It was clear that Anna, a sharp student and strong reader, knew quickly which words did not make sense. Although she still skipped endings here and there, she became more careful to include word endings on words read aloud—especially to her classmates. As the other students became more aware of endings and pointed out Anna's reading errors, she began to self-correct more consistently!

Name _____

More Mouse Messes

Look at illustrations in books from the Favorite Books Box.
Draw two different mouse messes below.

In the first box, draw and label single things
that could add to a mouse mess (like one bottle of ketchup).

In the second box, draw and label groups of "more-than-one things"
that could add to a mouse mess (like many pretzel sticks).

```
┌─────────────────────────────────────────────────┐
│                                                 │
│                                                 │
│                                                 │
│                                                 │
│                                                 │
└─────────────────────────────────────────────────┘
```

One thing then another can add to a Mouse Mess.

```
┌─────────────────────────────────────────────────┐
│                                                 │
│                                                 │
│                                                 │
│                                                 │
│                                                 │
└─────────────────────────────────────────────────┘
```

"More-than-one-things" can also add to a Mouse Mess.

Name _____

Smart Pets

Henry's dog Mudge is smart! Mudge rolled and drooled very well!
Do you have a smart pet or know of a friend's smart pet?
In the boxes below, draw four smart things this pet has done.
Don't forget to label each picture with an **-ed** word!

On the back of this paper, list other **-ed** words that could describe your pet on the first day you brought him or her home!

Name _____

Fill in the Endings!

On the lines below, write each root word with the ending shown above.

root word	-ing "I am..."	-ed "Yesterday I..."
1. write		
2. smile		
3. sing		
4. frown		
5. stop		
6. say		
7. walk		
8. see		
9. eat		
10. look		

Read the following sentences from Mouse Mess, Henry and Mudge Take the Big Test, and Five Little Monkeys Jumping on the Bed. Fill in the blanks with the missing ending. Use **-s, -es, -ed, or -ing**.

1. Mudge rolled over and start_____ to drool.

2. The mama call_____ the doctor. The doctor said, "No more monkeys jump_____ on the bed!"

3. Crackle-sweep, he rakes corn flake_____ and jumps into the pile he makes.

4. Tip_____ slip_____ , sugar falls. Pour and pat, make castle wall_____ .

5. One fell off and bump_____ his head.

Name _____

Happy Endings

Listen to the ending sentences read to you from a few favorite books. Listen for words that contain the endings of **-ed, -ing, -s,** or **-es**. Write each word in the appropriate box below using book spelling!

-ing words	**-ed words**

-s words	**-es words**

Books to Use:
Words With Happy Endings

Arthur's Thanksgiving by Marc Brown (Little, Brown & Company, 1983)

Blueberries for Sal by Robert McCloskey (Viking Press, 1976)

Five Little Monkeys Jumping on the Bed by Eileen Christelow (Clarion Books, 1989)

Five Little Monkeys Sitting in a Tree by Eileen Christelow (Clarion Books, 1991)

Good Books, Good Times! by Lee Bennett Hopkins (HarperCollins, 1990)

Henry and Mudge Take the Big Test by Cynthia Rylant (Bradbury Press, 1991)

If You Give a Moose a Muffin by Laura Numeroff (HarperCollins, 1991)

If You Give a Mouse a Cookie by Laura Numeroff (Harper & Row, 1985)

If You Give a Pig a Pancake by Laura Numeroff (HarperCollins, 1998)

Julius by Angela Johnson (Orchard Books, 1993)

Monster Mama by Liz Rosenberg (Philomel Books, 1993)

Mouse Mess by Linnea Riley (The Blue Sky Press, 1997)

Mrs. Katz and Tush by Patricia Polacco (Bantam Books for Young Readers, 1992)

The Paper Bag Princess by Robert Munsch (Annick Press LTD, 1980)

Sylvester and the Magic Pebble by William Steig (Simon & Schuster, Inc., 1969)

The Wizard the Fairy and the Magic Chicken by Helen Lester (Houghton Mifflin Company, 1983)

Snowballs, Gingerbread, and Other Special Words

Mini-Lessons

Snowballs, Gingerbread, and Rainbows

The Grouchy Ladybug's Blends

Give Me a Break!

Student Goals

To examine compound words

To identify words with initial consonant blends of *r, s,* and *l*

To separate words into syllables

Favorite Books to Use

The Grouchy Ladybug by Eric Carle
Dragon Gets By by Dav Pilkey
Snowballs by Lois Ehlert
The Gingerbread Boy by Richard Egielski
Where the Sidewalk Ends by Shel Silverstein
Something Big Has Been Here by Jack Prelutsky

Snowballs, Gingerbread, and Rainbows

GOAL To examine compound words

Compound words are great for beginning readers to focus on because they provide an opportunity to explore word combinations, use context clues for understanding meaning, and decode two words in one. Making word connections such as these helps students increase their awareness of the many different kinds of words they will encounter in their daily reading adventures.

This ability to decode or break words into smaller parts helps students see the parts in any word, compound or otherwise. For example, once students have recognized ball, identifying baseball, football and snowball will be easy because they are armed already with knowledge of half the word. Similarly, any word with all should be easy to tackle, so a word like wallpaper gives word detectives no trouble.

Breaking apart compound words allows students to explore the meaning of words. Defining a toothbrush as a brush used on teeth seems obvious enough. But what about a butterfly or a ladybug? Young children enjoy inventing definitions for compound words. Discussing and rationalizing words—even when there is no right or wrong answer—proves fun for beginning readers, lays the foundation for word curiosity, and in turn makes interested, engaged readers.

To get ready for this lesson, I select books from the Favorite Books Box containing titles with a compound word. I gather two packages of highlighting tape or wooden counting sticks and sticky tack (see tip on page 70). I line the blackboard chalk ledge with these books and gather the students around me, and we are ready to examine compound words from snowballs to ladybugs.

Book titles with compound words

▲ *Use highlighting tape to identify compound word parts: Highlight one or both of the two word parts to make these words stand out.*

> ### MANAGEMENT TIP
>
> If highlighting tape is difficult to locate in a local teacher supply store or catalog, try using colored counting sticks and sticky tack. Place a small ball of sticky tack on a counting stick and have students place the stick between the two words in each compound word on the book cover, to visually divide the two smaller words.

Mrs. L.: Look at these books from our Favorite Books Box and tell me if you can figure out what they have in common. I'll start with these two books: Lois Ehlert's *Snowballs* and Richard Egielski's *The Gingerbread Boy.* Try looking closely at the words *gingerbread* and *snowballs.*

David: They have two little words in them. *Snow* and *balls* and *ginger* and *bread.*

Mrs. L.: Exactly! There's a special name given to words that have two smaller words inside a bigger word. These words are called compound words. Let's use this highlighting tape to highlight the two different words inside each compound word on these book covers. What are the two smaller words in *snowballs*?

Allisa: *Snow* and *balls.*

Mrs. L.: Great. Let's take the orange highlighting tape and highlight *snow.* Let's highlight the word *ball* with blue. Now think about the meaning of the two small words in the compound word *snowballs.*

Olivia:	Well, snowballs are balls of snow.
Mrs. L.:	Exactly! Usually the two words are like this—the meaning of the two smaller words go together to mean something different. You don't picture snow and a soccer ball; you think of something completely different—a ball made of snow.
Katie:	Gingerbread is cake.
Carrie:	It's kind of like a bread.
Mrs. L.:	And there's ginger in it. So it's bread made with ginger. Let's use the highlighting tape to separate the two words *ginger* and *bread*.
	Take a look at Lois Ehlert's *Planting a Rainbow*. One of the words in this title is also a compound word.
Rachel:	*Rainbow*.
Mrs. L.:	Tell me about the meaning of *rainbow*.
Chris:	Well it's a bow of rain.
Anna:	Actually it happens after the rain, but it looks like a bow or a ribbon.
Mrs. L.:	Great. We'll highlight the compound word *rainbow*. Can you find another book with a compound word in its title?
Tommy:	*Dear Mr. Blueberry* has *blueberry* in it.
Mrs. L.:	Tell me about the two words in *blueberry*.
Abbey:	Blueberries are blue.
Mrs. L.:	Right—berries that are blue.
John:	*Some Birthday* doesn't have a compound word in it.
Stephanie:	Yes, it does—*birthday*. The day you were born is your birthday.
Mrs. L.:	Excellent. Billy, would you and Jonathan please highlight *birthday* for us? Any others?
Olivia:	*Holiday Handwriting School* has *holly* and *day* in it.
Carrie:	There's no day for holly. Besides it's not *holleeday*, it's *hol-i-day*.
Mrs. L.:	With a short vowel *i* sound.
Carrie:	Yes.
Greg:	No, *holiday* isn't the compound word. It's *handwriting*—writing you do with your hand.
Mrs. L.:	Yes. There's another hint about compound words—book spelling is used for both of the words that make up the compound word. *Holly* is spelled h-o-l-l-y not h-o-l-i.
Matthew:	Then it's not a compound word.
Mrs. L.:	Right. Let's highlight *handwriting*, not *holiday*.
Stephanie:	*Backstage with Clawdio* has *backstage*—a stage that is in the back.
Mrs. L.:	If you go backstage, you are in back of the stage where the people in the audience can't see you.
Greg:	Is *Clawdio* a compound word?
Mrs. L.:	What two words would make up the compound word?
Greg:	*Claw* and *dio*.
Mrs. L.:	What's a *dio*?

Greg: Oh. It must not be a compound word.

Mrs. L.: If the two words are not real words, then you don't have a compound word. *Claw* is a word but *dio* is not.

Alex: *'Twas the Night Before Thanksgiving* has a compound word in the title. *Thanksgiving*—giving thanks.

Greg: Why aren't the words just written as two separate words?

Alex: Because then *Thanksgiving* would be called "Giving Thanks Day."

Greg: No, I mean why don't we write it as *Thanks giving* with a space between the two words? When you read them they sound the same. I don't think I can remember all these two-word words.

Mrs. L.: Don't worry about remembering all these special compound words. As with most words in our language, reading them is the best way to learn. The more you read, the more words you will come in contact with and, therefore, the more words you will remember. And compound words take on a whole new meaning from the two smaller words. Picture a *toothbrush*—a brush that is used on your teeth. What you imagine when I say *toothbrush* is very different from a tooth and a brush. But put these words together, and you have a completely different thing. Let's find a few more compound words.

Molly: I read *The Grouchy Ladybug* last night before bed. *Ladybug* is a bug that's a lady.

Sara: I think *ladybug* is a compound word, but aren't there boy ladybugs too?

Marc: I think *ladybug* means a bug that looks like a lady.

Mrs. L.: Or maybe it's just a fun name that the person who discovered the bug invented. Maybe it's a word like *butterfly*—it's two real words put together to make a new word—a compound word—but the two words used don't necessarily fit the meaning of the new word.

Bobby: Well, a butterfly's not a stick of butter flying in the air!

Mrs. L.: I guess not! Some compound words make sense and some sound like invented words. The best thing about compound words is that they can make reading easier. If you recognize one of the smaller words in a compound word, chances are you'll be able to figure out the whole word.

Alex: Like *bug* in *ladybug*.

Mrs. L.: Yes. If you can read *bug*, you cover up this part and just figure out the other four letters.

Billy: L-a-d-y—lady.

Mrs. L.: If you use the beginning letter clue of *l* and then say *bug*, and use the rest of the words in the sentence to figure out the meaning clues, chances are you will know the word is *ladybug* pretty quickly.

Allisa: Or look at the picture of a ladybug if there is one!

Mrs. L. Great idea! Compound words are also helpful when you are writing. If you can write one of the words with book spelling, you only have to sound out the other word in the compound word. Let's finish highlighting these books with compound words in their titles. Let me put a few more on the board.

(We review several more titles, highlighting and discussing the compound words.)

Mrs. L.: You are excellent word detectives, really thinking about what these compound words mean. That's what being a reader is all about—understanding what you are reading. Words are interesting; they can make you curious and help explain all kinds of amazing things. Without compound words we wouldn't have babysitters, we would have "someone who comes to stay with children whenever they are alone." We wouldn't eat blueberries, we'd eat "berries that are blue." When you think about compound words this way, you realize how they save us time. Instead of having to say a bunch of extra words, we can say just one compound word. Other compound words are just fun words—

Carrie: Like ladybugs and butterflies!

Mrs. L.: I'm glad we have compound words; they make our world of words more interesting.

After our lesson, I invite the children to be word detectives at home. We copy a homework note that says:

> Look for a book with a compound word in the title. Bring this book to school.

The next day, we meet on the carpet to share the books brought in from home. *Goosebumps, rugrats* and *boxcar* are three new words from popular children's books that must be added to our list of Compound Words We Know.

Books with compound words from home

Using the book titles shared in class, I chart the compound words and meanings discussed in our original compound word lesson, then add our new discoveries as they are made. We soon realize that some definitions, *rugrats* and *goosebumps* for instance, must be invented using the two small words in the compound word. I copy the children's definitions on a chart.

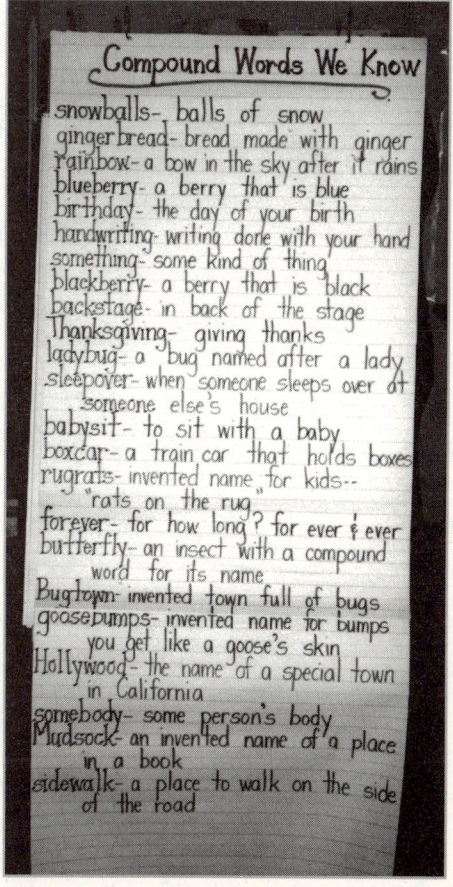

Compound word definitions ▶

Book Celebrations: Activities to Extend Learning

Independent Practice With Compound Words

For extra practice identifying compound words, I set up an independent work center where students read and identify compound words. Prior to introducing this center activity, I have students draw a picture of Dav Pilkey's Dragon character with 14 large spikes on his tail. I encourage students to make Dragon's outline and spikes as large as the paper allows since they will be writing a compound word on each of Dragon's spikes.

Using Pilkey's book *Dragon Gets By*, I have students work alone or in pairs to identify and then copy one compound word from the story onto each of Dragon's spikes. The 14 compound words in the story include some invented words for students to ponder, like *mailmouse* and *yardwork*, and others students infrequently see, like *doughnuts*, *wheelbarrows* and *cupboard*. Dragon's comical escapades make this center a fun place to extend learning about compound words.

For those students who love a challenge, have them copy the 14 compound words from the story as it is read aloud on a prerecorded tape. Not seeing the compound words in print makes this activity extra challenging. *Everything, newspaper, outside, inside, cupboard, bedtime,* and *afternoon* are familiar words that students have to identify as compound words.

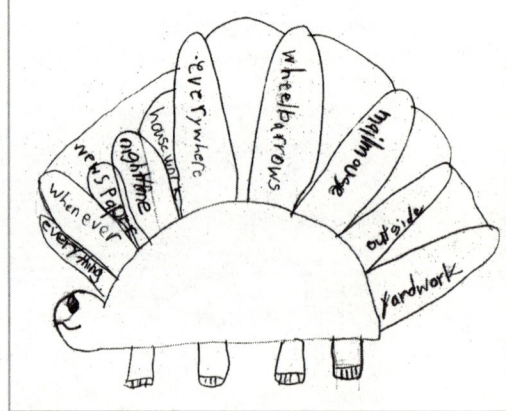

Dragon's compound words

Compound Word Assessment

The activity from this mini-lesson can be a quick assessment tool for identifying compound words and their two word parts. Have individual students meet you at the Favorite Books Box to look at more books with compound words in the titles. Students can use colored counting sticks or uncooked spaghetti to separate the two smaller words within each compound word on the book covers while you assess their compound word knowledge.

Henry and Mudge and the Bedtime Thumps by Cynthia Rylant and *My Rotten Redheaded Older Brother* and *Picnic at Mudsock Meadow*, both by Patricia Polacco, are three titles you may wish to have students explore.

The Grouchy Ladybug's Blends

MINI-LESSON 8

GOAL To identify words with initial consonant blends of *r*, *s*, and *l*

Consonant blends are clusters of letters that are helpful for students to recognize. As with word endings and the short words in compound words, recognizing blends helps kids break words into smaller parts for easier decoding. Practicing this skill on the words of a favorite text makes learning fun and relevant.

The Grouchy Ladybug by Eric Carle has many uses in the classroom. Whether used as a springboard for lessons on telling time, size, manners, shapes, or even initial consonant blends, this book is always a hit with beginning readers. After reading it several times "just for fun," I share it one more time to focus on the 25 words with initial consonant blends that happen to be a part of this beautiful book's text.

This lesson is flexible. Students can be asked to listen for one particular initial consonant blend or two or three at once. Before I teach the lesson that follows, I introduce my class to initial consonant blends, so I'm comfortable having my students identify r-blends, s-blends, *and* l-blends *in the same lesson. To prepare for this mini-lesson, I draw three ladybug shapes as a Venn Diagram on the board. (If you use another story, you can just draw a traditional Venn diagram with circles for recording the blends.) I label one ladybug as* r-blends, *another as* s-blends, *and the third as* l-blends. *As I read the story, I emphasize the words with initial consonant blends, making it easier for the students to identify them.*

<u>The Grouchy Ladybug</u> by Eric Carle ▶

To focus on one blend sound at a time, simply draw one ladybug (or circle) at a time on the board and ask students to identify words with this particular initial consonant blend. After you have explored *r-*, *s-*, and *l-blends*, a separate lesson can focus on putting all these kinds of words into the appropriate space of a Venn Diagram.

The Grouchy Ladybug lesson usually goes something like this:

Classifying words with blends

You may wish to have your students use their stop signs (see page 59) instead of clapping whenever a word with a blend is read.

Mrs. L.: The Grouchy Ladybug has a special word in its title.

Jonathan: Ladybug is a compound word.

Mrs. L.: I'm glad you remembered. Today we're going to be talking about another kind of special word that we haven't talked about before. We're going to talk about words that start with letters that blend together to make certain sounds. These words begin with *blends*.

Molly: Like in a blender?

Mrs. L.: Actually, that's a great way to think about these words. You know how you put ice cream and milk together in a blender—

David: To make a milkshake?

Mrs. L.: Yes! Well, before you blend these two ingredients together, you can tell the milk from the ice cream. But after you press the button, and the milk and ice cream whirl around in the blender, it's hard to tell the milk from the ice cream.

Carrie: Because they are all mixed up together.

Mrs. L.: Right!

Jonathan: What does ice cream have to do with words and reading?

Mrs. L.: Well, words with blends are a lot like making a milkshake, except that the two ingredients are letters and they blend together to make the sound in a word. The word *grouchy* is a word with a beginning blend sound. Can you guess which letters blend together to make the blend sound?

Sara: It's probably *g* and *r* even though I can hear both of the sounds in the words.

Mrs. L.: You're right. Just as you can still taste the ice cream and milk in a milkshake if you taste very carefully, if you say the word slowly, you will hear both sounds in the blended word. That's one of the reasons we are concentrating on blended sounds—when you read or write them, one of the sounds is often very easily missed, and the word tricks a reader.

Today we are going to listen for blended sounds at the beginning of words in *The Grouchy Ladybug* by Eric Carle. There are at least 25 words with blends in this story. Some of the blends have *r* in them, some have *s* in them, and some have *l* in them. *Grouchy* is an *r*-blend word, as we already said. *Blend* is an...

Stephanie: *L*-blend word.

Mrs. L.: You've got it! An *s*-blend begins a word like *spots*—like those on a ladybug—or *stand* or *slip*. Why don't you try repeating these words with blends: *Grrr-ouchy, grr-eat, prr-ance*.

Class: Grrr-ouchy, grr-eat, prr-ance.

Mrs. L.: St-and, st-op, sp-ot.

Class: St-and, st-op, sp-ot.

Mrs. L.: Bl-ends.

Class: Bl-ends.

John: Are those ladybugs on the board?

Mrs. L.: Yes. That's where we are going to record the words with blends. We'll put the words with *r*-blends on the first ladybug, the words with *s*-blends on the second ladybug, and the words with *l*-blends on the third ladybug. I'll read a page slowly, and you'll clap your hands when you hear a word that begins with a blend.

At five o'clock in the morning the sun came up. A fr-iendly—

Class: CLAP!

Billy: *Friendly* has a blend at the beginning.

Mrs. L.: Great! Where should I write this word?

Bobby: On the *r* ladybug.

Mrs. L.: Thanks. I'll keep reading.

A friendly ladybug flew in—

Class: CLAP!

Rachel: *Flew* has a blend. It goes on the *l* ladybug.

Mrs. L.: Great. I'll keep reading:

...from the left. It saw a leaf with many aphids on it, and decided to have them for breakfast.

Class: CLAP!

Tommy:	*Breakfast!*
Mrs. L.:	Good listening. Which ladybug should I use?
Tommy:	The *r*. *Brrr-eakfast.*
Mrs. L.:	This word is a tricky one to spell. It's *b-r*, then *e-a-k* for *break*—
Marc:	Then *fast* for the end.
David:	That word has a blend at the beginning and at the end—*st* at the end.
Mrs. L.:	Good thinking! We'll look for ending blends another day. Let's concentrate on beginning blends today. Here we go: But, just then a grouchy—
Class:	CLAP!
Mrs. L.:	You are quick! We already decided *grouchy* goes on the *r* ladybug so I'll write it under *breakfast*. Let's continue: …ladybug flew in from—
Class:	CLAP!
Billy:	*Flew*, but we already wrote that.
Matthew:	And *from*. *From* goes with *grouchy* and *breakfast* on the *r* ladybug.
Mrs. L.:	Excellent. We won't write *flew* again, but I'll write *f-r-o-m* under *grouchy*. How about if you smile when I read a word that we already recorded. It too saw the aphids and wanted them for breakfast. "Good morning," said the friendly ladybug. "Go away," shouted—
Class:	CLAP!
Mrs. L.:	You stopped me.
Jonathan:	You said *shouted*. That's an *s-blend* word.
Mrs. L.:	Oops, I think you've been tricked. You don't say *s* (I make the *s* sound)-*h* (I make the *h* sound)-*outed*. It's *sh-outed*. *Sh*, like *ch* and *th*, are special sounds (consonant digraphs), but they are not blends. I know this because when these two letters are put together, they make a completely different sound. Remember the letter sounds in blends can still be heard if you say the word slowly. Try saying *shouted*.
Class:	*Shshshshshs-outed.*
Abbey:	I can't hear the *s* or the *h*. I just hear *sh*.
Mrs. L.:	Good word detecting. Let's listen for more blends: …shouted the grouchy ladybug. "I want those aphids." "We can share them," suggested the friendly ladybug. "No. They're mine, all mine," screamed the—
Class:	CLAP!
Cassie:	*Screamed* has a blend.
Anna:	But you'll have to write it twice because it has *s* and *r*.
Mrs. L.:	Since this word is a three-letter blend—*s-c-r*—I'll write it in between the *r* and *s* ladybugs in this overlapping space. This space is to be used for words that have both letters in their blend.

Anna: The other space must be for l-s-blends.
Mrs. L.: Actually, they would be s-l-blends. I can't think of any words that start with l-s.
Matthew: Those two letters don't go together very well.
Mrs. L.: I agree. I'll keep on reading.

We continue reading and clapping, stopping to record blends on the ladybugs, and smiling when a recorded word is repeated. We stop after finding a few more words for each of the ladybugs, then take a few minutes during the next few days to find blends in the rest of the story. When we are finished our list of blends includes:

r-blends	s-blends	l-blends
friendly	sweetly	flew
breakfast	stepped	flippers
grouchy	stinger	
praying	stag	
front	sparrow	
trunk	skunk	
	starting	
s-_-r-blends	spotted	**s-l-blends**
screamed	snake	sleeping
stretching	started	slap
straight	still	
screeched		

These charts hang on the wall for weeks, and we add words to the chart as they arise in reading, writing, and speaking. When students are writing, I remind them to refer to the charts for help with a word beginning with a blend. In time, our lists of blends expands to include the following initial consonant blends:

bl, br, cl, cr, dr, fl, fr, gl, gr, pl, pr, scr, shr, sk, sl, sm, sn, sp, spl, spr, squ, st, str, sw, tr, and *tw.*

Soon the students begin to notice final consonant blends in reading and writing on their own. Before independent reading time on another day, I challenge students to find words that end with these consonant blends:

-dge, -ft, -nt, -nd, -ng, -nk, -pt, -sp, and *-st.*

Over time, as they continue to refer to the charts for comparing blended sounds in reading or writing, a growing awareness of blends becomes apparent in the students' improved spelling and word-attack strategies.

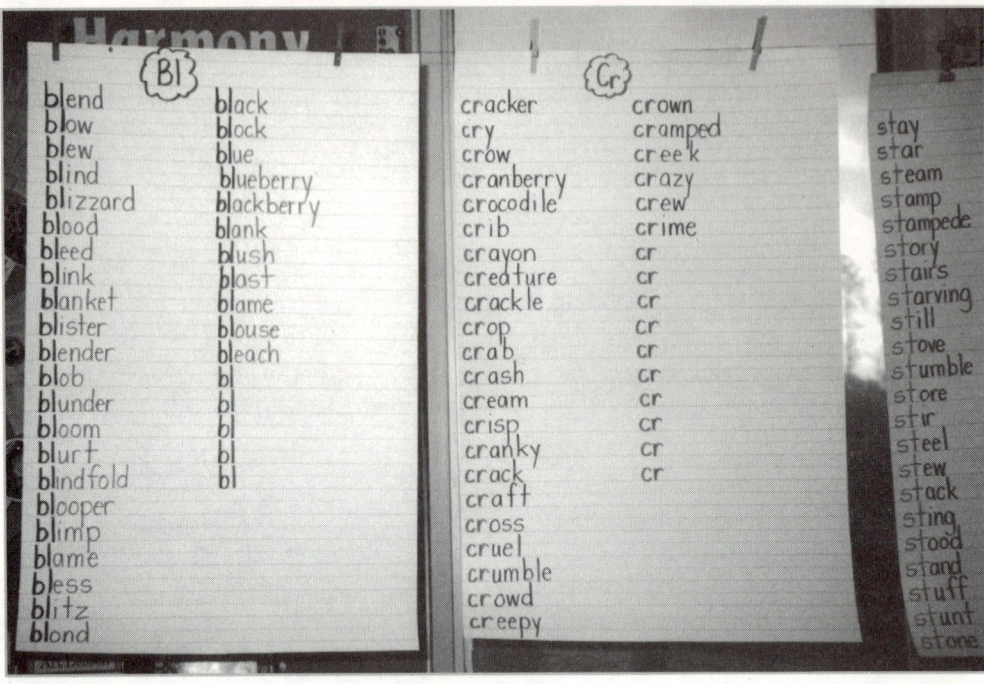
Blend charts

Book Celebrations: Activities to Extend Learning

More Grouchy Ladybugs

During silent reading times, I invite a group of students to sit near the Favorite Books Box and provide copies of Grouchy Ladybug Blends from page 91. The students search favorite books for words to record on their own Venn Diagram of *s-*, *r-*, and *l-blend* words. After the entire class has had a chance to search favorite books for blends, we meet together to share the many words they have discovered. We all agree that initial blends are common in words and therefore important for beginning readers to be familiar with.

Grouchy Ladybug blends ▶

Find-a-Blend Newspaper Game

Students enjoy racing against themselves in this timed find-a-blend activity. At a center area, I supply strips of newspaper cut into quarter-sheet or smaller sections, pencils or thin-tipped markers, and a timer (an egg timer or sand timer from a board game will work well). The charts of consonant blends hang within sight. Students are directed to circle all the words with blends they can find on their sheet of newspaper in the time given. You may wish to give students three minutes or so on their first try, then move to shorter intervals.

After counting and reading the blends to others at the center, students reset the timer to try again. Newspapers can be collected for your viewing or hung on a bulletin board labeled "Blends in the News."

Blends in the News ▶

Telling Time With The Grouchy Ladybug

All you need for this activity are individual student clocks (small "Judy Instructo clocks" are ideal) and an audiotaped recording of *The Grouchy Ladybug*. Students can listen to the story in small groups while moving the hands on the clock to match the time mentioned in the story. Students can show the time passing as the grouchy ladybug goes from one creature to another by moving the minute hand slowly around the clock dial until it shows the next hour. Students may take turns playing the "teacher," who checks the hands of all clocks to be sure they are in the right place at the right time. If necessary, this person can stop the tape to assist classmates.

MANAGEMENT TIP

Books and taped recordings are an excellent use of those extra book club bonus points! Unfortunately, not all books are available on tape. If you need an audiocassette recording of a story, try making the tape while your students are listening. Read a favorite story one more time, telling students you are making a recording. Remind students that any silliness will be recorded for all the world to hear—unless this is an invitation for silliness, of course. Remember to read the story with expression, and at the end of each page snap your fingers to let students know it is time to turn the page; pause for the "teacher" to do so.

Give Me a Break!

GOAL To separate words into syllables

One of my very favorite poems to share with boys and girls is "Sick" by Shel Silverstein. For 12 years, I have used this poem to help students get over their beginning-of-the-new-school-year fears. The children always giggle when little Peggy Ann McKay jumps out of bed, cured of all her imagined ailments as soon as she discovers it's Saturday.

In the mini-lesson that follows, I reuse the poem "Sick" to introduce the concept of syllables, another useful decoding technique that breaks words into smaller parts. The poem seems perfectly suited for this activity because it contains mostly one- and two-syllable words with occasional three- and four-syllable words used to make the rhythm just right. Another feature that makes it conducive to a lesson on syllabic units is the eight beats in every line. Eight is a reasonable number for beginning readers and writers to work with; all the words in each line of the poem, once broken into syllabic units, will add up to eight. Students enjoy discovering that Shel Silverstein shortened appendix to pendix to fit the eight-beats-per-line pattern.

After reading this poem many times with my students—snapping, clapping and tapping the rhythm—we discuss the humorous content of Peggy Ann's ailments and then do the following mini-lesson on breaking words apart into syllables. I simply grab an erasable marker and gather my students around a laminated, charted copy of the poem for a lesson that gives everyone a break from the usual lesson on identifying syllables in words.

<u>Where the Sidewalk Ends</u> by Shel Silverstein ▶

MANAGEMENT TIP

If your students have not had much practice playing with the beat of words, try using rhythm sticks. Call on volunteers to use the rhythm sticks to tap the beat while saying the words: *Mea-sles* gets two taps with the rhythm sticks; *in-sta-mat-ic* gets four.

Mrs. L.: Today I'd like to reread Shel Silverstein's poem "Sick" to show you something amazing I discovered about the words of this poem. Do me a favor and count on your fingers the number of beats in the first line like this (I count the beats on my fingers as I read):

"I can-not go to school to-day."

Stephanie: I got eight.

Mrs. L.: Smile if you agree. Let's try it again: "I can-not go to school to-day."

Tommy: I got eight, too. Is this the amazing thing you found out?

Mrs. L.: Let's try a few more lines and you can tell me if this is an amazing thing. Get your fingers ready: "Said little Peggy Ann McKay."

Billy: Eight again!

Mrs. L.: Here's the next line: "I have the measles and the mumps."

Anna: That's eight too. That is amazing!

Mrs. L.: You know, I think Shel Silverstein worked very hard at making all the lines of this poem work out to be exactly eight beats. In fact, this is one of the things that makes this poem so much fun to say—the beats. "I cannot go to school today said little Peggy Ann McKay, I have the measles and the mumps…" (I recite this much of the poem again with an exaggerated beat).

Bobby: It makes me want to snap my fingers, but I'm not very good at that.

Mrs. L.: Let's try another line just to make sure I counted correctly the first time. Ready: "A gash, a rash and purple bumps." Hold up your fingers to show me what you counted. Looks like eight to me! Now I'd like to let you in on a word power secret about the beats in words—they're called *syllables*. Try saying that.

Class: Syllables.

Mrs. L.: Right! Syllables are the smaller parts that a word is broken into that makes it have a certain number of beats. Syllables are excellent word clues for readers because they can help you figure out smaller parts of longer words. Shel Silverstein had to be an expert "syllable breaker" to make sure he had the eight beats, or syllables.

Bobby: He had to be a good counter, too. The first word was easy to count; *I* only has one letter.

Mrs. L.: *I* is a one-letter, one-beat word. One-beat words can't be broken apart into syllables.

Matthew: There's nothing to break!

Mrs. L.: Yes, you're right! I have a pen that will erase after I'm done writing on this laminated chart. If you tell me where to draw a line, I'll break the words apart into syllables on the chart. *Cannot* is the second word. How many beats in this word? Clap it: *Can-not*.

Sara: Two.

Mrs. L.: Any ideas of where I should draw the line in between the two syllables? Say the word to yourself.

Sara: I think it's *can* and *not*.

Carrie: Right in between the two words.

Mrs. L.:	That's it! Compound words are easy to break apart since the two words get separated. Now you can see the two syllables in this word. What about the next word, *go*?
Stephanie:	It has one beat so there's no place to break it.
Mrs. L.:	*To*?
Marc:	One beat, too.
Mrs. L.:	*School*?
Molly:	One beat.
Mrs. L.:	*Today*?
Katie:	Today has two. *To* and *day*.
Mrs. L.:	Wow! Another compound word. Let's look at this line now and count all the syllables and see if we get eight:

      I can-not go to school to-day
      1 2   3   4 5   6   7 8

Mrs. L.:	Great! Let's try another line. "Said little Peggy Ann McKay." What about the beats in *said*?
Allisa:	Just one.
Mrs. L.:	Right. How about *little*?
Alex:	*Lit-tle*. Two. So you need to draw a line.
Stephanie:	I think it goes in between the two *t*'s.
Mrs. L.:	This is one of the tricks to breaking words into syllables—when you have double consonants, the break is usually in between them. Try this trick on the next word: *Peggy*.
David:	It's has double consonants too! It's a two-beat word, and I think *Peg-gy* breaks at the *g*'s.
Mrs. L.:	You're right. *Ann*?
Chris:	One beat.
Mrs. L.:	*McKay*?
Rachel:	Two—the break is between the *m* and the *c*. *M-cKay*.
Mrs. L.:	You know this word works like a double consonant word. I don't think consonants are ever alone in a syllable; they always have another letter with them—usually a vowel. *McKay* is a special word because it's a name, and names often don't follow the rules.
Tommy:	I think *McKay* breaks after the *c*. *Mc-Kay*.
Mrs. L.:	I think you're right! Count this line, please: "Said lit-tle Peg-gy Ann Mc-Kay."
Class:	Eight!
Mrs. L.:	The next line is, "I have the measles and the mumps." Count all the words except *measles* and tell me what you get.
Class:	Six.
Mrs. L.:	So how many more beats do we need to make eight beats?
Class:	Two.
Matthew:	So *measles* must have two beats.

Mrs. L.:	You're right! *Mea-sles*. Where is the break?
John:	After the *l*.
Chris:	No, after the *s*.
Mrs. L.:	You know, this is a tricky one. I brought the dictionary in case this happened. Even teachers get stumped occasionally with syllables! Words in the dictionary are written in book spelling, of course, and they also are broken apart into syllables because this helps readers know how to say the words too. Remember, that's why I'm teaching you about syllables—examining the smaller parts of a word makes detecting easier. *Measles*—here it is *mea-sles*.
Chris:	I thought it would be *meas-les*.
Mrs. L.:	I wanted to check to be sure too. Let's count the syllables, or beats, in this line: "I have the mea-sles and the mumps."
Class:	Eight.
Mrs. L.:	Now let's pick out the tricky words in other parts of the poem to learn some other rules about breaking words into syllables. Remember the kind of flu Peggy Ann claimed to have?
Bobby:	*Instamatic*?
Mrs. L.:	Right! Let's try to break this word into syllables.
Anna:	*In* is first—
Katie:	Then *sta*, then *matic*.
Matthew:	No, it's *mat-ic*.
Mrs. L.:	Does it sound like three syllables or four syllables?
Matthew:	Four—*in-sta-mat-ic*. *Mat-ic* needs to be two separate syllables.
Mrs. L.:	Does the line go before or after the *t*?
Billy:	Before, I think.
Sara:	No, after the *t*.
Mrs. L.:	This is another tricky syllable break, but there is actually a way to remember which is correct. I'm thinking that if you put the *t* in the *-ic* syllable, then *m-a* is all by itself and that would make the *a* long, and it's not. So to show that it's *mat-ic*, we need to put the *t* with *ma* to make *mat*, and then *ic* is the last syllable.
Matthew:	*Mat* is a word, so it should stay together as a word, right?
Mrs. L.:	Consonant-vowel-consonant syllables that have a short vowel sound stay together in syllables too. In the word *mat*, *m* is a consonant, *a* is a vowel and *t* is a consonant. The *a* is short. If all this sounds tricky to you, don't worry. I'm introducing this syllable idea to you today, and we'll keep practicing syllables when we find interesting and challenging words. What is important to remember is that long words can be broken into smaller pieces to help you decode them like a real word detective. Let's practice a few more fun words together. Do you remember what Peggy Ann McKay says she did to her ankle?

(We continue through the poem, clapping the beat and breaking the words into syllables.)

For a ten-minute practice activity, I give small groups of students a stack of books and some colored counting sticks (dry spaghetti or yarn also works for this). Students place the sticks on the words of the book title to mark where the syllables break. *Yoko* by Rosemary Wells looks like *Yo-ko* with a stick in between *yo* and *ko*. *Jumanji* by Chris Van Allsburg becomes *Ju-man-ji* with two sticks dividing this title. Group members check one another's work for accuracy, and I am called to settle any disagreements with a dictionary in hand. Critical thinking is used since words like *Jumanji* and *Yoko* are not found in our dictionary, and we are forced to rely on what we've learned from "real words" to guide us.

Giving words a break

Following our free-exploration time, we meet again briefly to discuss any tricky words encountered in small groups. One group shared the discovery that endings are often by themselves in syllables and used the example of *Planting a Rainbow* by Lois Ehlert. *Planting* was broken so that the root word *plant* stood alone. Another group supported this theory with the book *Working Cotton* by Sherley Anne Williams. I record a page in our word power notebook, which highlights our findings:

Giving Words a Break—SYLLABLES

If a word:
- has double consonants, it breaks between the double letters;
- is a compound word, it breaks between the two words;
- has an ending, the ending usually stands alone;
- fits the c-v-c pattern, the c-v-c parts stays together in the syllable.

Breaking words apart into syllables is important for helping students spell and attack words a chunk at a time. Aside from the fact that longer words seem less intimidating when broken into syllabic units, reflecting on what can be learned by breaking words apart can also be enlightening for beginning readers.

Book Celebrations: Activities to Extend Learning

Spaghetti Syllables

Dry spaghetti or yarn, word power notebooks, and a pile of favorite books are all that is needed to give students additional practice in syllable breaking. These tangible objects make breaking words fun for beginning readers. Have students record "broken" words (with lines drawn between syllables) on a page in their word power notebooks. This allows you to check students' understanding of syllables. A separate page for "words that cannot be broken" gives students a place to record one-syllable words. Remind students to check the dictionary whenever they encounter a difficult word to break.

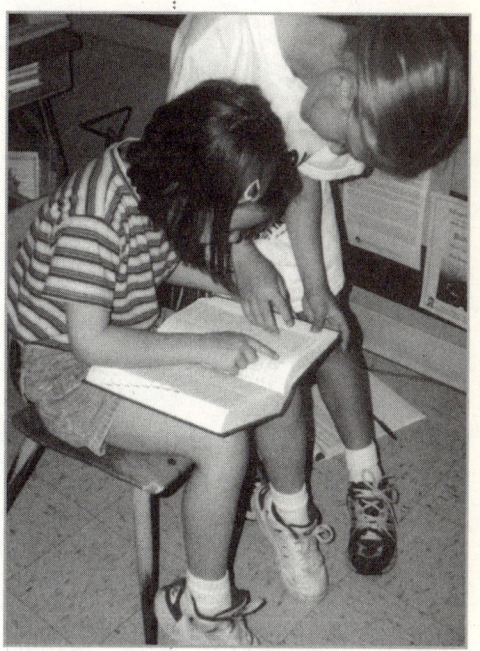

Double-checking a tricky word ▶

Using Syllables to Improve Spelling

After reading a story for Read Aloud, choose a sentence to copy on the board and break into syllables. Explain to your students that writers use knowledge of syllables to help them spell difficult words and to make sure that all of the parts of a word have been written. The following sentence from *Tulip Sees America* by Cynthia Rylant illustrates how beats help the flow of a story—even when it's not a poem.

> The skies in Nebraska. They are everything.
> They are vast and dark and low and ominous.
> And a tiny Beetle feels even tinier, driving beneath them.
> It feels a little afraid (11).

Use a sentence such as this to show how words like *Nebraska* and *ominous* could be spelled more easily when broken apart or sounded out by syllables. For additional practice, use colored chalk and call on volunteers to break the words into syllables. Or pass out rhythm sticks to test the beats of individual words.

Working together on breaking syllables ▶

You Can't Beat Poems

When it comes to working with syllables, you can't beat poems! Many, like "Sick," have a built-in checking system at the end of each line. Students can work alone or in pairs to identify the pattern of beats per line, then use their new knowledge of syllables to test an author's pattern. Provide rhythm instruments and charted poems with a distinct beat for a free exploration center on syllable counting.

Some fun poems for exploring are Jack Prelutsky's "The Zoo Was in an Uproar," with its 7-6-7-6 line pattern (*Something Big Has Been Here*, pages 62–63) and "Oh, Teddy Bear" with its 8-7-8-7 pattern (*The New Kid on the Block*, pages 110–111). Try Shel Silverstein's "Eggs Rated" for nonsense word breaking (*Falling Up*, page 149) or "Magical Eraser" for identifying varying numbers of beats per line (*Where the Sidewalk Ends*, page 99).

Syllable Assessment

Here are two fun activities to test your students' understanding of syllable breaking. During an independent work time, call on individual students to come and tap or clap words that you have written on laminated index cards or on a lap-sized white board or chalkboard. Asking students to draw a line where they heard the break tests their understanding of syllables in print. On another day, provide students with a copy of Syllables Count (see page 92) for a pencil-and-paper assessment of syllable counting using Shel Silverstein's poem "Hug O' War" (*Where the Sidewalk Ends*, page 19).

Tapping syllables ▶

Word Power Assessment: Special Words

Make copies of the letter from the president of "Petgifts, Inc." to Marc Brown's *Arthur* (found on page 93) to assess your students' understanding of syllables, consonant blends, and compound words. Ask students to circle consonant blends and place a squiggly line under compound words found in the letter. Have them circle two three-syllable and two two-syllable words and draw lines through the words to indicate the syllable breaks. You may wish to read the letter sentence by sentence while the students listen for and mark all the special words.

Carrie, Grade 2

HELPING A FLUENT READER BECOME A BETTER SPELLER

Carrie is a very careful, methodical reader who reads with great expression and uses strategies when faced with unknown words. Carrie's creative writing demonstrates attention to detail and includes lots of descriptive language. Carrie's spelling, however, is not as accurate as it could be, given her acceleration in other areas. Although she receives perfect scores on nearly every Friday spelling test, this book spelling did not carry over into her own story writing. Because she is a fluent reader and writer, I knew she was familiar with the appropriate spelling of many words and decided it was time to help Carrie proofread her work more carefully.

I copied the following sentences from James Marshall's *Rats On the Roof and Other Stories* onto a small lap-sized white board, adding inappropriate spaces between the compound words and misspelling words with blends. I was ready to begin my one-on-one time with Carrie.

> Early one morning in May, a mouse sperang out of bed,
> danced in to the bath room, and stepped under an ice-cold shower.
>
> Otis and Sophie Dog had just tucked them selves in for the night
> when the sound of little dancing feet and shrill musical instruments
> reached their suleepy ears.

Mrs. L.: I've copied two sentences from our favorite book, *Rats On the Roof and Other Stories* by James Marshall. But I'm afraid I've made a few mistakes.

Carrie: They look fine to me.

Mrs. L.: They did to me, too, but then I realized I misspelled a few words. I was hoping you would help me fix them.

Carrie:	Sure—I'm pretty good with compound words.
Mrs. L.:	How about consonant blends?
Carrie:	They're a little harder for me.
Mrs. L.:	We'll look at them together. You know, when James Marshall was writing *Rats on the Roof*, there's a good chance he made a few spelling mistakes too.
Carrie:	He was probably concentrating on getting the ideas down on paper.
Mrs. L.:	I agree, and that's the most important part of writing because you don't want to forget your ideas. But after he was finished getting his ideas written down, I know he went back to check his spelling. This was important so that the people reading his book could understand what he was trying to say in his stories. Please read the first line.
Carrie:	Sure. "Early one morning in May, a mouse…" I'm not sure what this word is—s-p-e-r-a-n-g.
Mrs. L.:	That may mean it's misspelled. Try reading the rest of the words in the sentence and then name the sounds in this word.
Carrie:	"Early one morning in May, a mouse blank out of bed." Sper… Sprang out of bed. That word's supposed to be sprang.
Mrs. L.:	Oops—I added an extra letter when I copied it down.
Carrie:	Is it just *spr-ang*? I'll take out the extra e. I'm pretty sure *bathroom* is a compound word.
Mrs. L.:	You're right again! Would you please change *bath room* so that it is one word instead of two? The rest of this sentence seems fine to me. Do you agree?
Carrie:	Yes.
Mrs. L.:	I see two more changes that need to be made.
Carrie:	*Sleepy* does not have a u because it's not *sul-eepy*. It's just *sl-eepy*.
Mrs. L.:	Right again! There is one more misspelled word in the second sentence.
Carrie:	I don't see any. What kind of word? Give me a hint.
Mrs. L.:	These two words should be one compound word.
Carrie:	I know it—*themselves*.
Mrs. L.:	Right! You just did some excellent proofreading. Now that I know what a good job you can do with blends and compound words, I'd like you to reread your stories after you have written them to make sure you have spelled all the words that you can with book spelling. This makes it easier for you and for others to read the words that you write.

Carrie worked hard at proofreading her stories—"just like James Marshall," she explained. Over time, her spelling improved with proofreading. Although she still made many errors when initially getting her ideas down on paper, she saw the importance of checking her work and made the changes that needed to be made with all kinds of "special words."

Name _____

Grouchy Ladybug Blends

Use the Ladybugs below to record words that begin with **s-**, **r-**, and **l-blends**.

Look at the books in the Favorite Books Box and challenge yourself to find at least five of each kind of blend. How many **sl-** and **s_r-blends** can you find?

Hint: The two blends in the title of this recording sheet have been done for you.

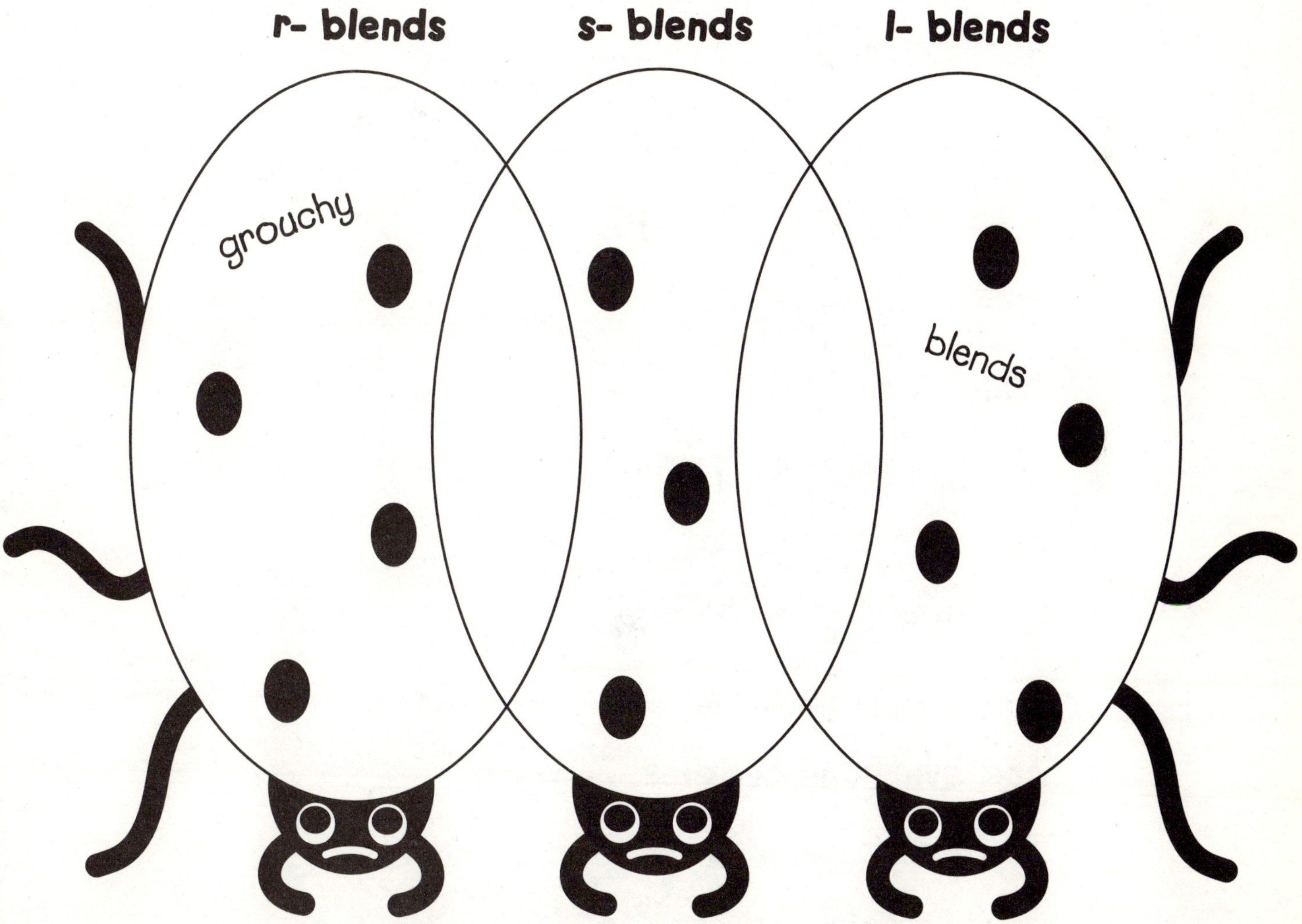

r- blends   **s- blends**   **l- blends**

grouchy

blends

Use this space for other words with blends.
How many different kinds of blends can you find?

Name _____ Date _____

Syllables Count!

Draw lines to break the words below into syllables.

Use your fingers to help you count the beats in each line of the poem "Hug O'War" by Shel Silverstein (*Where the Sidewalk Ends*, page 19).

Record this number at the end of each line. Do you begin to see a pattern?

HUG O' WAR

I will not play at tug o'war.   _____

I'd rather play at hug o' war.   _____

Where everyone hugs   _____

Instead of tugs,   _____

Where everyone giggles   _____

And rolls on the rug,   _____

Where everyone kisses,   _____

And everyone grins,   _____

And everyone cuddles,   _____

And everyone wins.   _____

 Add the numbers from each line together to get a total number of syllables for the entire poem!

TOTAL _____

Name _____ Date _____

Dear Mr. Arthur Aardvark,

    We just know your dog, Pal, will wag his tail with joy when he sees the new and improved Treat-Timer 5000, doggy ear plugs and complimentary box of special dog snacks available at your favorite pet store for just $19.99.

    Simply place the ear plugs on your pet, flip the switch and watch the treats fly everywhere! (Optional safety doggy goggles are available for $5.00 plus tax.) Dogs love chasing the new rainbow colored treats made from 100% gingerbread. Don't forget to buy our new blueberry flavored doggy toothpaste and toothbrush to wash away these tasty sweets from your pooch's teeth! (Simply enclose an additional $5.00.)

    Our customers' happiness is our number one concern, and we regret any problems you had with our product. Please fill out the card and send it along with your money today!

                                  Sincerely,

                                    Oliver T. Moneymaker

                                  Oliver T. Moneymaker
                                  President of Petgifts, Inc.

Books to Use: Special Words

Arthur Babysits by Marc Brown (Little, Brown and Company, 1992)

Arthur's Birthday by Marc Brown (Little, Brown and Company, 1989)

Arthur's First Sleepover by Marc Brown (Little, Brown and Company, 1994)

Blackberry Ink by Eve Merriam (William Morrow and Company, 1985)

Backstage With Clawdio by Harriet Berg Schwartz (Alfred A. Knopf, Inc., 1993)

Dear Mr. Blueberry by Simon James (Aladdin Paperbacks, 1991)

Dragon Gets By by Dav Pilkey (Orchard Books, 1991)

The Gingerbread Boy by Richard Egielski (HarperCollins, 1997)

The Grouchy Ladybug by Eric Carle (HarperCollins, 1977)

Henry and Mudge and the Bedtime Thumps by Cynthia Rylant (Macmillan Publishing Company, 1991)

The Holiday Handwriting School by Robin Pulver (Macmillan Publishing Company, 1991)

Jimmy's Boa and the Big Splash Birthday Bash by Trina Hakes Noble (Dial Books for Young Readers, 1989)

Jumanji by Chris Van Allsburg (Houghton Mifflin Company, 1981)

My Rotten Redheaded Older Brother by Patricia Polacco (Simon and Schuster, 1994)

The New Kid on the Block by Jack Prelutsky (Greenwillow Books, 1984)

Picnic at Mudsock Meadow by Patricia Polacco (G.P. Putnam's Sons, 1992)

Planting a Rainbow by Lois Ehlert (Harcourt Brace & Company, 1988)

Some Birthday by Patricia Polacco (Simon and Schuster Books for Young Readers, 1991)

Something Big Has Been Here by Jack Prelutsky (Greenwillow Books, 1990)

Snowballs by Lois Ehlert (Harcourt Brace & Company, 1995)

Somebody and the Three Blairs by Marilyn Tolhurst (Orchard Books, 1990)

There's Something in My Attic by Mercer Mayer (Dial Books for Young Readers, 1988)

Tulip Sees America by Cynthia Rylant (Blue Sky Press, 1998)

'Twas the Night Before Thanksgiving by Dav Pilkey (Orchard Books, 1990)

Where the Sidewalk Ends by Shel Silverstein (Harper and Row, 1974)

Working Cotton by Sherley Anne Williams (Harcourt Brace & Company, 1992)

Yoko by Rosemary Wells (Hyperion Books for Children, 1998)

CHAPTER 4
Planting a Rainbow of Long and Short Vowels

Mini-Lessons

Student Goals

Mini-Lessons	Student Goals
The Rainbow Rule	To examine words that follow the long vowel rule: When two vowels are together, the first vowel is long
The Five Little Monkeys' Bossy *E* Rule	To examine words that follow the silent *e* long vowel rule
Max, Fox, Henry, Mudge, and Little Critters' Short Vowel Sounds	To investigate words with short vowel sounds

Favorite Books to Use

Planting a Rainbow by Lois Ehlert
Five Little Monkeys Sitting in a Tree by Eileen Christelow
Max's Dragon Shirt by Rosemary Wells
Henry and Mudge in the Green Time by Cynthia Rylant
Me Too! by Mercer Mayer
Fox on the Job by James Marshall

The Rainbow Rule

GOAL To examine words that follow the long vowel rule: When two vowels are together, the first vowel is long

Vowel sounds are always tricky for beginning readers. Not only do vowels have both a short and a long sound assigned to them, but the short sounds are difficult for inexperienced readers to distinguish. Long vowel sounds are the sounds I like to introduce first to my students since they "say their names." But it's knowing whether to use the long or short vowel sound when decoding a word that makes these sounds confusing. An early beginning reader once pointed to the vowels in the unknown word we were attacking together and said, "I'll skip those letters. I never know the right sound."

I remembered chanting a catchy phrase as a second-grade student myself: "When two vowels go walking, the first one does the talking, the second one does the walking." This fairly reliable rule boosted my confidence as a beginning reader and gave me a kind of test to perform on words anytime I saw two vowels walking together in a word. I decided to present this rule to my first- and second-grade readers in the hope that it would give them a measure of confidence when faced with vowels. Knowing that anytime two vowels are side by side in a word, the long vowel is the first sound to be tried is a useful decoding strategy.

I searched the Favorite Books Box for title words with two vowels walking together—some that follow the rule and some that break the rule. Lois Ehlert's book Planting a Rainbow was the first book I found, and *rainbow* became a key word for describing this rule. Prior to the lesson, helpers copy the Rainbow Rule on the board for me; then I am ready to introduce it to my students in a mini-lesson that goes something like this.

"When two vowels go walking, the first one does the talking, the second one does the walking."

Mrs. L.: I have the Favorite Books Box with me today because we are going to be word detectives and hunt for more special words.

Bobby: Words with endings?

Mrs. L.: No, today we're going to become experts on vowels. Tell me which letters are vowels.

Carrie: A, e, i, o, and u.

Mrs. L.: You're off to a great start. A, e, i, o, and u are special letters for a couple of reasons. What if I told you vowels are so important that there is at least one vowel in every single word in the English language.

Greg: I'd say they must be pretty special letters!

Mrs. L.: I agree. Vowels are also special letters because every vowel has two sounds, not just one sound like the consonants t, s, or r.

Matthew: That's what makes them hard to figure out—there are two sounds to choose from!

Mrs. L.: I want to teach you a rule that vowels are supposed to follow. First, let's talk about the two sounds that vowels make. The two sounds for vowels are called *long* and *short* sounds. We'll save the short vowel sounds for another day.

The rule we'll be talking about today is a long vowel rule which I call the Rainbow Rule. The long sound of a vowel is the one that says the vowel's name. The long sound for *a* is "aaaay." The long sound for *e* is "ee." The long sound for *i* is—

Class: "Eye."

Mrs. L.: The long sound for *o* is—

Class: "Oh."

Mrs. L.: And the long sound for *u* is—

Class: "You."

Mrs. L.: Excellent! Some helpers wrote the Rainbow Rule on the board for us. Let's read it:

Class: When two vowels go walking,
the first one does the talking,
the second one does the walking.

Rachel: The one that talks, what does it say?

Mrs. L.: That vowel says its name: *a, e, i, o,* or *u*.

Anna: The vowel that walks just walks, right?

Mrs. L.: Right. I call this the Rainbow Rule because *rainbow* is a word that has two vowels walking together—one talking vowel and one walking vowel. Look at the title of Lois Ehlert's book *Planting a Rainbow*. Tell me the two vowels in the word *rainbow*, please.

Class: A and i.

Chris: There's an *o* too.

David: But it's all by itself. They have to be walking together, don't they?

Mrs. L.:	That's right. So in the word *rainbow*, the first vowel is *a*, so *a* does the talking. That's why the word is *r-aaa-inbow*.
Alex:	You don't hear the *i* saying anything at all.
Abbey:	It's just walking along in the word.
Mrs. L.:	Say the Rainbow Rule as I point to the letters in *rainbow*.
Class:	When two vowels go walking, the first one does the talking, the second one does the walking.
Mrs. L.:	Let's test this rule on some other words. I'll show you a book. You look at the title for two vowels walking together. When we find these letters, we'll test the Rainbow Rule. How about *A Chair for My Mother* by Vera Williams?
Stephanie:	*Chair* is a rainbow word. The *a* talks but the *i* just walks.
Mrs. L.:	Excellent. I'll put this book on the chalk ledge under the rainbow rule. Look at *Dear Mr. Blueberry* by Simon James.
Cassie:	*Dear* is a rainbow word.
Olivia:	So is *blueberry*.
Mrs. L.:	Wow! Two rainbow words in one title! Let's test them both.
Katie:	*Dear* follows the rule. The first vowel is *e*. *D-eee-ar*. The *e* says its name.
Stephanie:	And the *a* doesn't say anything. It just walks.
Mrs. L.:	More wonderful detecting. Now let's look at *blueberry*. The two vowels are?
Class:	*U* and *e*.
Tommy:	I don't think that word follows the rule.
John:	I do.
Billy:	Me too.
Mrs. L.:	Let's say the word slowly. *Bl-uuu-eberry*. The *u* sound may not sound as clear as the *a* in *rainbow*, but I think the *u* does say its name.
Abbey:	Well, the *e* doesn't say anything, that's for sure.
Mrs. L.:	I agree. I'll put this two-rainbow-word book with the others that follow the Rainbow Rule. Here's another book to examine: *Henry and Mudge in the Green Time* by Cynthia Rylant.
Bobby:	*Green* has two vowels. It passes the test—the *e* says its name.
Matthew:	But how do you know the second *e* isn't the one saying its name?
Bobby:	No, it's the first vowel.
Mrs. L.:	You know, we really don't have any way of knowing which *e* is doing the talking. I guess we'll just have to believe this vowel isn't cheating on the test, and we'll let it pass. Is that fair?
Class:	Yes.
Mrs. L.:	How about *The Bookshop Dog*, also by Cynthia Rylant.
Olivia:	*Bookshop* is the two-vowel word. But I don't think this word is a rainbow word.

Mrs. L.: It's not the "Boke-shop" Dog, is it?

Class: No!

Mrs. L.: Then I agree that this word does not pass the rainbow-word test. Let's write "Words That Break the Rainbow Rule" on the board and put *The Bookshop Dog* under it. *Just Plain Fancy* by Patricia Polacco is the next book to test.

Carrie: *Plain* is the rainbow word, and since the *a* says its name, it passes the test.

Mrs. L.: Great! How about *Just a Dream* by Chris Van Allsburg?

Jonathan: *Dream* is the two-vowel word. The *e* says its name so it's a rainbow word.

Mrs. L.: You're right. Let's try a few more. Here's *Owl Moon* by Jane Yolen.

Tommy: *Moon* has two *o*'s in it. I think the *o* says its name.

Carrie: No, it doesn't. It's not a "mone," it's a m-ooo-n. Like a cow says "moo."

Tommy: I guess it's not a rainbow book.

Mrs. L.: This one fails the rainbow test. How about *The Grouchy Ladybug* by Eric Carle?

Molly: *Grouchy* is the word with two vowels. The first vowel is *o* so it should say its name.

Jonathan: No, it doesn't say *o*. It's not The "Grochy" Ladybug.

Mrs. L.: More excellent word detecting. I think you are becoming experts on the Rainbow Rule. Now every time you come to a word in your reading that you are unsure of, if that word has two vowels together, the first thing you should do is…

Stephanie: Make the sound of the first vowel.

Marc: If the word breaks the rule it doesn't help.

Mrs. L.: In a way it does. If the long sound for a particular vowel doesn't work, then you know to try the short vowel sound. And remember perhaps the biggest word detective clue…

Katie: Making sense when you are reading.

Mrs. L.: Exactly! Anytime you try to read a word that you aren't sure of, read the other words in the sentence, skipping the unknown word. You can get very helpful clues from what makes sense in place of the unknown word.

Let's take a few minutes to copy the Rainbow Rule on special bookmarks to help you remember it later today, tomorrow and, hopefully, forever!

After each word that follows the Rainbow Rule, I have students read the rule aloud as I point to the vowels to reinforce it. When we're finished with our discussion, I send the students to their seats, pass out copies of page 120, and have them copy the Rainbow Rule on the bookmarks. After decorating them with a rainbow, kids copy five rainbow words from the books on the chalk ledge onto the back of the bookmarks.

Rainbow Rule bookmark

During silent reading that day, students take time to list other rainbow words they encounter in their reading. A group of students sits near the board to record words that follow the Rainbow Rule. At the end of silent reading, we take a few minutes to share the rainbow words discovered and recorded. The students' knowledge of words with long vowel sounds has been greatly expanded after our Rainbow Rule mini-lesson and this simple independent follow-up activity.

Words that follow the Rainbow Rule ▶

Book Celebrations: Activities to Extend Learning

More Rainbow Words

To provide students with the opportunity to search for and record other "two-vowels-together" words, I set up a Rainbow Word Center. Extra copies of the bookmarks and crayons and the Favorite Books Box are placed in a designated area. Students search the books for more rainbow words and copy them in rainbow colors on additional bookmarks during free time. These additional bookmarks can be secured together using a hole punch and yarn to look like a store-bought bookmark with fancy strings.

Breaking the Rainbow Rule

I encourage students to be on the lookout for words that break the Rainbow Rule. When they discover a word such as *grouchy, meadow,* or *noises,* I invite them to record these words on a chart titled "Words that Break the Rainbow Rule." Each word must be double-checked to make sure it has two vowels walking together without a long vowel sound before it can be recorded on the chart. When we have an extra minute—waiting for lunchtime or the buses at the end of the day—we retest these Rainbow Rule breakers.

Every Word Has a Vowel

To prove that all words have vowels in them, I write a short note to the students on the board explaining some aspect of our school day. After discussing the message, I explain how this would be a perfect opportunity to see if every word has a vowel. I move my finger slowly under each word, beginning with the first word in the note. I ask the students to stop me every time I come to a vowel. When they say "stop," I circle that vowel. The students soon realize that even one-letter words like *I* and *a* have vowels, which helps prove the importance of learning the two sounds of each vowel.

Nonsense Rainbow Words

Nonsense words are a great way to reinforce any reading skill—if students apply the newly learned skill, they can read a word the way it was intended to be read. The added dimension of nonsense makes the lesson playful for the children. I begin by inventing five or so nonsense words that follow the Rainbow Rule: *xaekin, treabuv, ploaz, miijjaffy,* and *plueff* are some examples of words we sound out together. For added fun, give a reason for inventing the words, such as inventing a new cereal or toy whose name must follow the Rainbow Rule. Try double rainbow words such as *bleapwiit* or *sasseatruef* as an added challenge. Then have students create their own nonsense rainbow words for a toy or snack they have invented.

The Five Little Monkeys' Bossy E Rule

GOAL To examine words that follow the silent *e* long vowel rule: When a word ends in silent *e*, the other vowel should be long.

I always tell my first graders that silent e has a very important job: to tell the other vowel in the word to say its name. One day as I was introducing this idea to the class, a little boy chimed in, "that's because e is bossy." What a clever way to explain the silent e rule, I thought. For the rest of that year, and for all future years, silent e will be known as Bossy E.

Bossy E's role is fairly straightforward, and as I've mentioned before, beginning readers feel comfortable knowing that there are some rules that are usually followed in this crazy language of ours.

I begin by sharing my invented names for the characters in *Five Little Monkeys Sitting in a Tree* by Eileen Christelow. The names—Kate, Pete, Mike, Joe, and Sue—all end in Bossy E, of course. I write the letters of each name on Post-It™ Notes, writing the e in red, then scramble each name. Through role playing and hands-on exploration of words, students quickly learn a word power lesson with the help of Bossy E and the Five Little Monkeys.

<u>Five Little Monkeys Sitting in a Tree</u> by Eileen Christelow ▸

Mrs. L.:	We've been talking about long vowel sounds, and today I'd like to tell you about another long vowel rule. Once you know about this rule, figuring out words with this special letter will be a snap! To help show you how this works, I need the help of the five little monkeys from the book by Eileen Christelow.
Anna:	Is this rule like the Rainbow Rule?
Mrs. L.:	Well, it does help us know when a vowel should be long. This rule is called the silent *e* rule. Sometimes, like in the word *five*, words end in an *e* but this *e* is not pronounced. We say *five*, not "fiv-ee." Instead, the *e* has another important job in the word—*e* tells the other vowel in the word to say its name.
John:	Sounds like that is a Bossy E to me.
Mrs. L.:	That is a perfect way to think of silent *e*. It may be silent, but it certainly is bossy. We'll have to call this letter Bossy E from now on—that's much more fun. In the word *five*, the vowel that Bossy E tells to say its name is…
Class:	I.
Mrs. L.:	Right. To show you how Bossy E works, I'm going to need your help. Yesterday I was reading *Five Little Monkeys Sitting in a Tree* and I thought it would be fun to give the five little monkeys names—of course, all of their names must follow the Bossy E rule. I invented names for all five monkeys but then I accidentally scrambled up the letters. Will you help me put them back in order? I remember the first little monkey's name because he looks like a "Mike" to me. Let's spell this together.
Stephanie:	Well, we know it ends in Bossy E, so put that last.
Billy:	It starts with M and then an *i* sound and a *k* sound.
Stephanie:	So it's M-i-k-e.
David:	Right.
Mrs. L.:	Thank you! Now the Post-It Notes are in order. Could I please have four volunteers? Alex, would you be the M?
Alex:	Sure.
Mrs. L.:	Please stick this M on the front of your shirt. Rachel, John, and Molly, why don't you be *i*, *k*, and *e*. Please put the letters on your shirts and line up in order to spell Mike's name for your classmates. This will help you see Bossy E's job in a word. Alex, you're first. Please say the sound that M makes.
Alex:	"Mmm."
Mrs. L.:	Now *i* is next. But Rachel, you can't say anything until Molly, our Bossy E, comes and taps you on the back and reminds you to say your name. So Molly, would you give *i* a reminder, please.
Molly:	[Bossy E taps Rachel on the shoulder and says,] I, say your name.
Rachel:	I.
Mrs. L.:	Now John will say the sound for *k*.
John:	"Kh."

Mrs. L.: Great! Now try it again, this time without my help.
Alex: "Mmm."
Molly: I, say your name.
Rachel: I.
John: "Kh."
Sara: They all did their jobs in the word.
Mrs. L.: Yes, they did. I'll put Mike's name on the board with the letters in the right order.

(We follow the same process for the rest of the monkeys, Pete, Sue, Kate, and Joe.)

Mrs. L.: That was quick! Our five little monkeys are Mike, Pete, Sue, Kate, and Joe. Five little Bossy E's. You know if these names did not have Bossy E, they would be completely different words. E makes the other vowel long and without the e, the other vowels would be short.
Stephanie: Pete's name would be *Pet*.
Mrs. L.: Exactly! Mike would be....
Sara: *Mick*.
Mrs. L.: Yes. Kate would be *Kat* with a short *a* sound.
Greg: What would Joe be?
Mrs. L.: Well, short *o* sound is *o* so it would be—
Stephanie: *Jaw*.
Mrs. L.: Anytime you read a word that has a silent, or Bossy, *e* at the end of it, you should first try to sound out that word using a long vowel sound.
Anna: And the *e* doesn't make a sound at the end of the word.
Mrs. L.: Good reminder. Let's test Bossy E in these four book titles. *Arthur Writes a Story* by Marc Brown, *Seven Blind Mice* by Ed Young, *Flute's Journey* by Lynne Cherry, and *How a Book Is Made* by Aliki. Tell me the word in each title that ends in Bossy E, please.
Greg: *Arthur Writes a Story* doesn't have a word that ends in Bossy E.
Mrs. L.: Actually, if you remove the ending on one of the words, it does.
Carrie: *Writes*—take off the *s*. The Bossy E tells the *i* to say its name.
Mrs. L.: Excellent. Tell me about another title.

(We discuss the rest of the titles.)

Mrs. L.: Once again you are being excellent word detectives. If you use the Rainbow Rule and the Bossy E Rule, you will have great helpers in figuring out words you don't know. Let me show you one more book— *Mouse Mess* by Linnea Riley.
Sara: *Mouse* ends in Bossy E.
Mrs. L.: Say the word *mouse*, and see if *e* is bossy in this word.

David: It's not "mose." E doesn't boss the o.

Katie: O and u walk together.

Billy: Then *mouse* breaks two vowel rules.

Jonathan: Maybe *mouse* should be on a Breaks the Bossy E Rule poster and our Words That Break the Rainbow Rule poster.

Mrs. L.: You're right. I wanted to show you this word because there will be words like *mouse* that break the rules. Word detectives always use other clues to help them make sense of what they are reading.

Stephanie: The picture of the mouse gives you a hint about the mouse in the story.

Mrs. L.: Pictures are very important clues. Hardworking word detectives have a lot to remember when it comes to learning new words. Keep practicing and using everything you know about words to help you when you are faced with a challenging new word.

Role playing "Bossy E"

Book Celebrations: Activities to Extend Learning

Monkey Names: Reinforcing the Bossy E Rule

Working in small groups, students design posters depicting each monkey—Mike, Pete, Sue, Kate, and Joe. Students may enjoy using black crayon and watercolors to outline and then color in the poster. I have each group mark the monkey's name with a long vowel line and then draw an arrow from the silent *e* to this long sounding vowel—another way to depict how *e* tells the other vowel to say its name. We display the five posters in the classroom with the words:

When a word ends in Bossy *E*, the other vowel should be long.

An artist's "thumbnail" sketches of Sue and Joe

As students come in contact with other Bossy *E* words, these words are copied on index cards and glued to the appropriate chart hanging below each poster. Words with long *a* are added to Kate's chart, and words with long *o* are added to Joe's chart, for example.

Role-Playing Nonsense

On word cards, write nonsense Bossy *E* words such as those listed below. Small groups of three or four students role-play how these words work, as demonstrated in the lesson above. Provide time, Post-It Notes, and markers for students to invent their own nonsense Bossy *E* words, then record these words that follow the silent *e* rule. When you have a few extra minutes, role-play these student-invented words as a class.

Bossy E Nonsense Words

flope	naze	queze
pripe	zube	bluxe

Max, Fox, Henry, Mudge and Little Critters' Short Vowel Sounds

GOAL To investigate words with short vowel sounds

Each year, to introduce my students to the confusing world of short vowel sounds, I would hang pictures of an apple, elephant, igloo, olive, and umbrella on the chalk ledge. Then one day I was reading a Henry and Mudge book with a student during silent reading. We came to a word with short u and I said, as she stumbled over the vowel sound, "Say the u sound like in M-u-u-u-dge's name." She smiled and said "Mudge is more fun to say than umbrella." I decided to identify four other book characters to represent the short vowels and retire my fading pictures. Mudge, along with Henry, Max, Little Critters, and Fox became the appointed short vowel representatives. The students remembered these friendly points of reference much more easily than olives and igloos. Use your own favorite characters to help students remember short vowel sounds.

As with all the mini-lessons in this book, adapt the lesson to suit your individual needs, perhaps introducing one vowel and corresponding book character a day or each week. You may wish to follow up each individual vowel lesson with extension activities to

(Continued)

Our short vowel book characters ▶

reinforce specific vowel skills, then finish with a lesson that compares all five vowels. The following lesson introduces all five vowels but also makes a useful review or assessment activity. I have found that using this lesson as an overview of all the sounds helps students see the full picture of vowels and is not too overwhelming—even for beginning readers. It's important to keep in mind that knowledge about short vowels takes place over time, with lots of repetition and encouragement.

To prepare for this short vowel mini-lesson, I stock a bag with objects such as those listed below and collect books depicting short vowel characters to display as points of reference. I am now ready for a lesson that helps my students classify objects according to their short vowel sounds.

Short Vowel Surprise Bag

a small box of crackers
a stuffed cat
a hat
an apple

Book: Max's Dragon Shirt by Rosemary Wells
(or any book with a title character whose name has a short a)

a wrapped present
a stuffed elephant
a plastic or hard-cooked egg
a letter in an envelope

Book: Henry and Mudge in the Green Time by Cynthia Rylant (or any book with a title character whose name has a short e)

I
a gift
a toy pig
a toy fish
a picture

Book: Little Critters Me, Too! by Mercer Mayer (or any book with a title character whose name has a short i)

O
a sock
a lollipop
a stuffed dog
a box

Book: Fox on the Job by James Marshall (or any book with a title character whose name has a short o)

U
a toy truck
a small umbrella
a cup
a plastic bug

Book: Henry and Mudge and the Wild Wind by Cynthia Rylant (or any book with a title character whose name has a short u)

In the lesson that follows, vowels in boldface represent the sound of a given letter as it is pronounced in the word, not the vowel's name.

Mrs. L.: When you are reading or sounding out a word, five letters can cause readers some confusion. The sounds of these letters sound very much alike.

Stephanie: I bet you mean the vowels.

Mrs. L.: You got it! When you are sound-spelling a word, getting the vowel sound correct can make the difference in being able to read that written word again later. When you are reading a word, knowing what sound to give each vowel can help you figure out the word more easily. Vowel sounds are tricky but very important in reading and writing words. I have five friends here with me today who can help you learn the short vowel sounds—the vowel sounds that do not come right out and say their names like the long vowel sounds. Look at the five books on the chalk ledge. Do you recognize any of the faces on the covers?

Jonathan: Fox and Max.

Katie: Henry and Mudge.

Olivia: The Little Critters.

Mrs. L.: You know them all! Now please tell me the vowel in each of their names. I'll write the vowels in big letters above each book.

Cassie: Fox has an *o*.

Sara: Max has an *a*. Henry has an *e*.

Tommy: Mudge has two vowels. One is Bossy E.

Cassie: But his name breaks the Bossy E rule. The *u* doesn't say its name.

Mrs. L.: Right. So, it's not a long *u*; it's a short *u*. What about the Little Critters?

Carrie: I think *little* is a word like *Mudge*—the *i* doesn't say its name. It breaks the Bossy E rule too.

Mrs. L.: Yes, it does. And the second *e* in *critters* is part of the *er* sound at the end so that *e* has a job. I think the *i* is the main vowel sound in *little* and *critters*. I wonder if you could help me put these characters in ABC order according to the short vowel sounds in their names.

David: A is the first letter of the alphabet, so it must be the first vowel too. So *Max* is first.

Marc: E is next, so *Henry* is the next one.

Rachel: I is next, so it's *Little Critters*.

Anna: U—no *o* is next, in *Fox*.

Molly: *Mudge* is last.

Mrs. L.: Great job. A, e, i, o, u is ABC order for vowels. Now help me say each character's name, pausing to give the vowel sound extra effort: M-**aaa**-x, for example.

Class:	M-**aaa**-x.
Mrs. L.:	The short sound for *a* is **aaa** like M-**aaa**-x. Max is now our official short vowel friend for the letter *a*. Try *Henry*.
Class:	H-**eee**-nry.
Bobby:	I bet *Henry* is our official short vowel friend for *e*.
Mrs. L.:	You guessed it! Try *Little Critters*—you need to say this vowel sound twice.
Class:	L-**iii**-ttle Cr-**iii**-ters.
Jonathan:	Our official friends for short vowel *i*.
Class:	F-**ooo**-x.
Class:	M-**uuu**-dge.
Mrs. L.:	*A*, *e*, *i*, *o*, and *u* are five of the trickiest sounds in our alphabet. With the help of these five favorite book characters, you can become experts on the short vowel sounds in no time at all—with a little practice of course.
	Let's start practicing right now using this surprise bag. You can take turns choosing things from the bag. We'll decide what vowel sound is used in each item. Then we'll give the items to the character with the same short vowel sound. Who would like to choose the first item? Abbey?
Abbey:	It's a sock.
Mrs. L.:	S-**oo**-ck. Which character has the **o** sound? Max, Henry, Little Critter, Fox, or Mudge?
Abbey:	I think it's Fox.
Mrs. L.:	Smile if you agree with Abbey. I do, too. Good work! Fox gets the sock. We'll put the sock on the floor under Fox's book. Next item. Billy, would you choose something from the bag, please?
Billy:	Yum! Crackers!
Mrs. L.:	Cr-**aaa**-ckers.
Billy:	Max for sure.
Mrs. L.:	Smile if you agree. Great word detecting. I'll give the crackers to Max. He looks a little hungry, don't you think? Alex, would you choose a short vowel item from the bag?
Alex:	It's a birthday gift.
Mrs. L.:	How nice! G-**iii**-ft. Who gets the gift?
Tommy:	Fox.
Carrie:	I think it's Little Critter.
Anna:	Me, too.
Mrs. L.:	Let's test this one: Say g-**ii**-ft. Say F-**ooo**-x. Do they sound alike?
Bobby:	No, I think it's Little Cr-**iii**-ters.
Mrs. L.:	Try g-**ii**-ft, L-**ii**-ttle Cr-**iii**-ters.
Class:	G-**ii**-ft, L-**ii**-ttle Cr-**ii**-ters.
Mrs. L.:	That's the one. Short *i* sound. I'll give this gift to the Little Critters.

Anna: You know I thought that was a present, not a gift.

Matthew: That's the same thing.

Mrs. L.: But they do have different vowel sounds. Anna, look closely in the bag; I think there's another wrapped box. We'll call this one a present.

Matthew: Then the present has to go to Henry. They both have short *e* in them.

Mrs. L.: That's right. I'll give the present to Henry. You're getting very good at detecting short vowels. Let's see what other surprises we can find inside this short vowel bag.

(We continue classifying objects by their short vowel sounds.)

Mrs. L.: If you keep these characters in mind and compare the sound you need for sound-spelling or the sound you need to try when reading a new word, they can help you remember the sounds that short vowels make.

Classifying objects by short vowel sound ▶

When we are finished, we have classified the following words according to their short vowel sound:

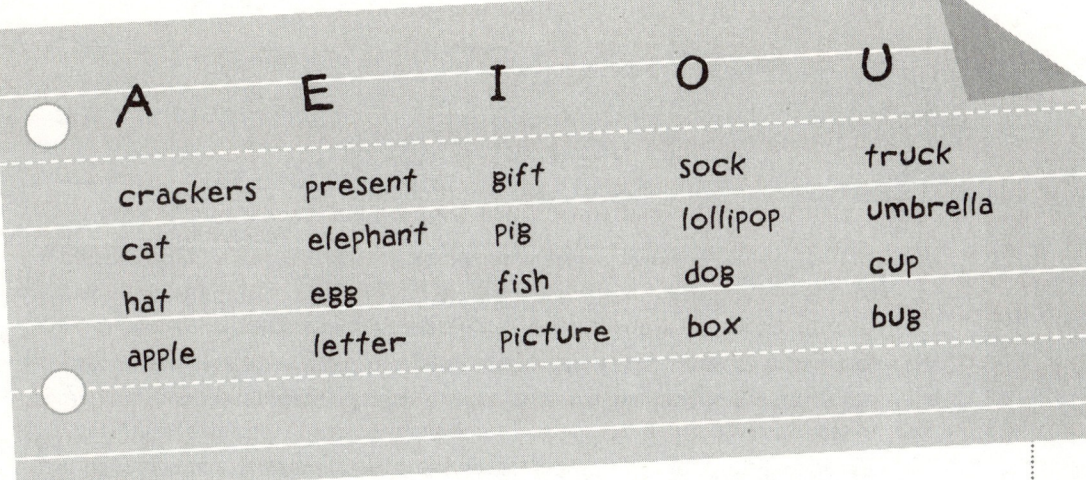

A	E	I	O	U
crackers	present	gift	sock	truck
cat	elephant	pig	lollipop	umbrella
hat	egg	fish	dog	cup
apple	letter	picture	box	bug

I end the lesson by writing these short-vowel words on the board, as shown above. Throughout the day, we add extra words to our list to reinforce these vowel sounds. Students' names, subjects such as math, and events such as lunch and a special gathering all get added to our growing list of short-vowel words. As our list grows, so does the children's confidence and knowledge of short vowel sounds.

Book Celebrations: Activities to Extend Learning

Short Vowel Books

For an ongoing short vowel project, we construct short vowel booklets. Each short vowel is placed at the top of five separate pieces of paper along with drawings of the designated short vowel character. Max, Henry, Little Critters, Fox, and Mudge (or whatever characters you choose) reinforce the short vowel sound for each letter. Kids decorate a construction paper cover and staple it to the short vowel pages to make a book.

Next, students think of examples of other words with short vowel sounds to be included in the booklet—Max might have an apple, an alligator, and an ant on his page, for example. The children may choose to draw their own items or cut out pictures of these short-vowel words from magazines and place them on the appropriate pages. I usually find that a combination of the two, hand-drawn and magazine pictures, works best. You may wish to set a limit of at least five pictures per vowel page. Remind students to talk about words they are unsure of before gluing them in the booklet!

This activity is great for those students who finish another project and have a few extra minutes on their hands. It also makes a nice center activity during a readers' workshop or similar book time.

Illustrating short vowel o ▶

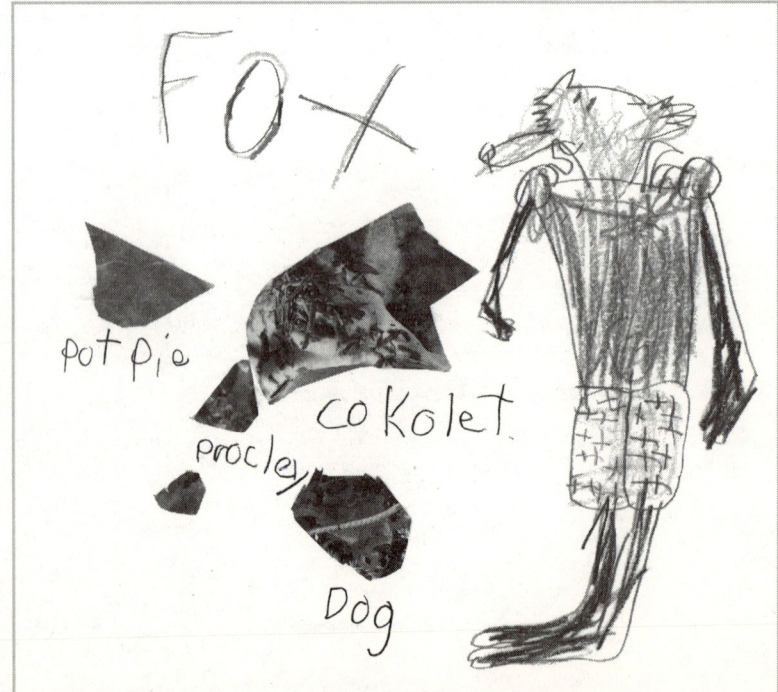

Writing With Short Vowels

Using the pages in their short vowel books, students choose a favorite character and write a short story using as many short vowel words as possible.

One s<u>u</u>nny day, M<u>u</u>dge was m<u>u</u>nching on m<u>u</u>ffins when s<u>u</u>ddenly...

Students then highlight and count all the emphasized short vowels in the story to see how many different short-vowel words have been used. During sharing time, classmates make tallies on slips of scrap paper for each particular short vowel sound as authors take turns reading their vowel-packed stories.

Sign Language and Handmade Vowels

Sign language is an effective tool to use with beginning readers. Using hands allows students to feel letters and the corresponding sounds, making the letters more tangible. I usually begin teaching sign language at the beginning of the school year, using the book *The Handmade Alphabet* by Laura Rankin, to reinforce letter-sound relationships.

Each day, we take five minutes or so to practice our signs and the sounds they make. I say, "The sound for *a* is 'a-a-a'" while forming the letter *a* with my hands. When we begin talking about short vowels, I use sign language to help students "sound out" vowels with their hands as well as their ears and mouths. Using the signs has become automatic, and the students love this added twist to reading and writing. Sign language also provides a quiet way for students to respond in a group situation: "Show me in sign language what vowel sound is in the word *duck*." A Sign Language Alphabet chart (1993 Frank Schaffer Publications, Inc.) hangs near our gathering space for quick review of the signs from *A* to *Z*.

Children practicing vowels with sign language ▶

Word Power Assessment: Another Bag Full of Vowel Sounds

Use a bag filled with objects that have names beginning with short and long vowel sounds along with the recording sheets found on pages 121–122 to assess your students' understanding of this word power skill. As you display objects from the bag one at a time, students may draw a quick picture or sound-spell words to record each item shown in the appropriate space provided. Use objects such as those listed below and others from your classroom to make this fun-filled assessment effective for your students.

SHORT AND LONG VOWEL OBJECTS TO USE:
hat, sock, truck, cup, apple, egg, picture, ring, crayon, pen, note, pine cone, acorn, leaf, toy trumpet, toy flute

Student Snapshot

Jonathan, Grade 2

HELPING A BEGINNING READER WITH VOWEL SOUNDS

Jonathan is a second-grade "haphazard" reader. I call him this because Jonathan relies on guessing rather than strategies for figuring out unknown words. When it was time to assess his understanding of short and long vowel sounds, Jonathan explained, "When I come to vowels, I just skip them." Although many words can be decoded relying solely on consonants along with context and picture clues, the importance of vowel sounds becomes apparent to students when they are asked to spell words on their own accounting for all the sounds. For Jonathan, this request finally helped him see the need to concentrate on learning the short vowel sounds.

Using the short and long vowel objects listed above and a lap-sized white board, I sat down with Jonathan to classify and spell words with their appropriate vowel sounds.

Mrs. L.: I have some objects that I would like you to help me organize by vowel sound.

Jonathan: I skip vowel sounds in words.

Mrs. L.: Sometimes that may work. But it's important that you learn these sounds in case you ever get stuck on a word. Vowel sounds might be just the help you need to decode or figure out that word. And sometimes the vowel sound is the only difference between two words. Think of the words *cat, cot,* and *cut.* Without other words around them, you have to rely on the vowel sound to figure out how to read each word!

Jonathan: Well, I know the long vowel sounds.

Mrs. L.:	Great! Let's work on some short vowel sounds too, so that you're an expert on all the vowel sounds. On the white board, I have written the vowels two times—once for the long sounds and another time for the short sounds. Choose an object from the bag and we'll decide where you should write the name of that object.
Jonathan:	This one's easy. It's a pine cone. It's long *i*. Is this a rainbow word?
Mrs. L.:	Actually, it's a Bossy E word. In fact, both words are Bossy E words, *pine* and *cone*—both vowels use Bossy E to say their names.
Jonathan:	I heard it that time—*cone* has long *o*. I'll write this word and underline the *o*.
Mrs. L.:	Nice printing, Jonathan. Try another object from the bag.
Jonathan:	It's a horn.
Mrs. L.:	Musicians call this a *trumpet*. Do any vowels say their names?
Jonathan:	No, it must have a short vowel sound.
Mrs. L.:	Look at the short vowel friends to help you find the right sound for spelling *tr-uuu-mpet*.
Jonathan:	Sounds like *Muuudge*. So it's short *u*.
Mrs. L.:	Excellent! I think there's another short vowel sound in *trumpet*.
Jonathan:	*Pet* has short *e*. I already know how to spell that word. It must be *t-r-u-m-p-e-t*.
Mrs. L.:	Great spelling. You can write this word twice.
Jonathan:	Once under *u* and once under *e*.
Mrs. L.:	Let's try sorting a few more objects. You're becoming an expert on vowel sounds.

Long Vowel Sounds

a	e	i	o	u
cr<u>ay</u>on	l<u>ea</u>f	p<u>i</u>ne cone	pine c<u>o</u>ne	fl<u>u</u>te
<u>a</u>corn			n<u>o</u>te	

Short Vowel Sounds

a	e	i	o	u
h<u>a</u>t	trump<u>e</u>t	p<u>i</u>cture	s<u>o</u>ck	tr<u>u</u>mpet
<u>a</u>pple	<u>e</u>gg	r<u>i</u>ng		tr<u>u</u>ck
	p<u>e</u>n			c<u>u</u>p

Jonathan continued selecting objects and classifying them according to vowel sounds. Spelling the words on the white board reinforced the importance of knowing all the vowel sounds. I knew our time spent together had been successful when Jonathan commented, "I guess I don't need to skip the vowels anymore—I'm pretty good at them!"

The Rainbow Rule:

When two vowels go walking, the first one does the talking, the second one does the walking.

Make a Rainbow Bookmark for recording words that follow the Rainbow Rule:

1. On the blank side of your bookmark, copy the Rainbow Rule, then decorate with a rainbow. Cut out the bookmark.

2. Use the numbered lines to record words that follow the Rainbow Rule that you find in your favorite books.

Rainbow Words

1. _____
2. _____
3. _____
4. _____
5. _____
6. _____
7. _____
8. _____
9. _____
10. _____
11. _____
12. _____
13. _____
14. _____
15. _____

Name _____

Short Vowel Assessment

a   e   i

o   u

121

Name _____

Long Vowel Assessment

a

e

i

o

u

Books to Use: Word Sounds

Arthur Writes a Story by Marc Brown (Little, Brown and Company, 1996)

The Bookshop Dog by Cynthia Rylant (The Blue Sky Press, 1996)

A Chair for My Mother by Vera Williams (Greenwillow Books, 1982)

Dear Mr. Blueberry by Simon James (Aladdin Paperbacks, 1991)

Five Little Monkeys Sitting in a Tree by Eileen Christelow (Houghton Mifflin Company, 1991)

Flute's Journey: The Life of a Wood Thrush by Lynne Cherry (Harcourt Brace & Company, 1997)

Fox on the Job by James Marshall (Dial Books for Young Readers, 1988)

Fritz and the Mess Fairy by Rosemary Wells (Dial Books for Young Readers, 1991)

The Handmade Alphabet by Laura Rankin (Dial Books, 1991)

Henry and Mudge and the Wild Wind by Cynthia Rylant (Bradbury Press, 1993)

Henry and Mudge in the Green Time by Cynthia Rylant (Bradbury Press, 1987)

How a Book Is Made by Aliki (Harper & Row Publishers, 1986)

Just a Dream by Chris Van Allsburg (Houghton Mifflin Company, 1990)

Just Plain Fancy by Patricia Polacco (Bantam Doubleday Dell Publishing Group, 1990)

Max's Dragon Shirt by Rosemary Wells (Dial Books for Young Readers, 1991)

Me Too by Mercer Mayer (Golden Books Publishing Company, Inc., 1997)

Mouse Mess by Linnea Riley (The Blue Sky Press, 1997)

Owl Moon by Jane Yolen (The Putnam Publishing Group, 1987)

Planting a Rainbow by Lois Ehlert (Harcourt Brace & Company, 1988)

Seven Blind Mice by Ed Young (Philomel Books, 1992)

Extending and Reviewing Word Power Skills

Mini-Lessons

Same Words, Different Meaning
Same Meanings, Different Words

A Noun Pizza

Review With *Yoko*

Student Goals

To investigate homonyms and synonyms

To identify a noun as a person, place, or thing

To review word power skills

Favorite Books to Use

Arthur's TV Troubles by Marc Brown
Rats on the Roof and Other Stories by James Marshall
Something Big Has Been Here by Jack Prelutsky
Pete's a Pizza by William Steig
Where the Sidewalk Ends by Shel Silverstein
Yoko by Rosemary Wells
Chrysanthemum by Kevin Henkes

Same Words, Different Meanings
Same Meanings, Different Words

MINI-LESSON 13

GOAL To investigate homonyms and synonyms

Homonyms are challenging for beginning readers, but after kids have gained confidence in their reading ability through word power lessons, they are ready to tackle these tricky words. The following lesson introduces homonyms while building kids' awareness about English. I've also found that it generates curiosity about words and gets them excited about language. To prepare for the lesson, I chart sentences from our Favorite Books Box using incorrect homonyms (see chart and note on next page). Two *for* to, hear *for* here, *and* inn *for* in are a few of the homonym mistakes I include.

After gathering the children for the mini-lesson, the first thing I do is read the sentences without allowing them to see the printed chart. Everything sounds fine. Then I invite them to read each sentence with me under the guise of wanting to discuss these "words that paint pictures." There's usually at least one student in the class who recognizes the misused homonym in the sentence. If no one recognizes an error, I simply say, "Something doesn't look right here. I think I misspelled this word. Oh, no, I think I misspelled a lot of words!" I make sure to impress on the class that there are some words that sound exactly the same when they are spoken but look very different when they are written and have different meanings too.

Even having to point out the homonyms introduces students to their existence and so makes them better word detectives. The lesson in which we explore these "same-sounding words with different meanings" goes something like this.

Learning about homonyms and synonyms ▶

125

★ A NOTE ABOUT THE HOMONYM CHART: I have included the titles and authors of each sentence used and have underlined each misused homonym on the homonym chart for your convenience. When charting the sentences with homonyms for classroom use, I do not include the title and author or underline the homonyms but read each sentence from its book as the students read from the chart. It is important for the students to know the origin of each sentence; it demonstrates the relevance of homonyms to the real world of words!

Favorite Sentences With Homonyms

Mr. Putter creaked, his <u>hare</u> was thinning, and he was a little deaf, <u>two</u>. —Mr. Putter and Tabby Pour the Tea by Cynthia Rylant

Eyes peeped <u>threw</u> keyholes. —Night Noises by Mem Fox

Did you ever <u>here</u> of Mickey, how he heard a racket in the <u>knight</u> and shouted "Quiet down in <u>their</u>!" —In the Night Kitchen by Maurice Sendak

"Tell me again how you called Granny and Grandpa <u>write</u> away, but they didn't <u>here</u> the phone because they sleep like logs."
—Tell Me Again About the Night I Was Born by Jamie Lee Curtis

They had left <u>they're</u> worn-out old planet to start a <u>knew</u> life in a <u>knew</u> world. —The Wump World by Bill Peet

...all the way back to their snuggly beds, <u>wear</u> they huddled and cuddled their own little teds. —Where's my Teddy? by Jez Alborough

"Wow," said Arthur. "Pal needs <u>won</u> of those." —Arthur's TV Trouble by Marc Brown

"Do I really have to?" asked Arthur as he <u>eight</u> his cereal.
—Arthur's Halloween by Marc Brown

Were the dinosaurs mistaken <u>four</u> dragons? Or did pirates <u>steel</u> them away? —Whatever Happened to the Dinosaurs? by Bernard Most

They kicked up their <u>heals</u> and ran like mad.
—The Day the Goose Got Loose by Reeve Lindbergh

"How would you like to <u>meat</u> your <u>deer</u> sweet mother?"
—Lyle Finds His Mother by Bernard Waber

"<u>Know</u> more drawing on the sheets, Tomie!" —The Art Lesson by Tomie dePaola

Mrs. L.: Last night I was looking through the Favorite Books Box and found some great sentences. These sentences all paint word-pictures of what is happening in the story. I've turned the chart backward so you can't see it. I want you to close your eyes and, while I read, paint a picture in your mind of what is being described. When I'm done, you can tell me which sentence you liked the best. I'll hold up each book to show you where I found each sentence.

(I read the charted sentences shown on page 126 to the class.)

Mrs. L.: Did these words paint pictures in your mind of what was happening?

Anna: Yes, I like the one where the grandma and grandpa don't hear the phone ring because they sleep like logs. I bet they're snoring too.

Mrs. L.: Could be! That's from *Tell Me Again About the Night I Was Born*. I'll turn the chart around so you can see the sentences now. Here's that sentence. Oh, my, it seems I've made a spelling mistake in this sentence. Does anyone else notice it?

> Tell me again how you called Granny and Grandpa write away, but they didn't here the phone because they sleep like logs.

Tommy: Is that how you spell *write*?

Mrs. L.: Yes, it is.

Sara: That doesn't look right.

Mrs. L.: That's exactly how *write* is spelled—if you are talking about how to print something with a pencil or crayon.

Jonathan: No, they called granny and grandpa, they didn't write to them.

Mrs. L.: Oh, that's right! Wow, I said that word *right* again. But wait a minute—are you sure I'm saying the right word *right*? And if we're not talking about writing with a pen or pencil, what other kind of *write* is there?

Sara: The other one you just said—that Jonathan was *right* about something.

Matthew: When you're not wrong, you're *right*.

Mrs. L.: I understand—*right* and *write*. But how do you know if I'm saying the *right* word?

Abbey: Yeah, they sound the same.

Mrs. L.: Please say the kind of *write* that you do with a pencil.

Class: Write.

Mrs. L.: Now say the word *right* that tells me I'm not wrong but *right*.

Class: Right.

Mrs. L.: I'm not sure if you said the right *right*.

Molly: We did! You have to believe us.

Mrs. L.: Let me see if I have this straight: The words *right* and *write* sound the same when you say them.

Sara: But they are not spelled the same way.

Mrs. L.: Oh! So I should have someone spell these words for me to make sure the correct word is being used.

David: I'll spell them.

Mrs. L.: Okay, please spell the word *right*.

David: W-r-i-t-e.

Mrs. L.: I'm sorry, that's not the *right* I wanted you to spell.

Carrie: You have to give him a hint about the kind of *right*.

Mrs. L.: Then what you're telling me is that when two words sound exactly the same, it's the words in the sentence that give clues about which way the word should be spelled. David, please spell the word *right* that I'm using in this sentence: "It's fun thinking of the *right* words to spell."

David: I don't know how to spell that *right*!

Stephanie: It rhymes with *light*. Look at the word sign by the light switch.

David: Oh. It must be r-i-g-h-t.

Mrs. L.: I'll write *right* on the board. I've been playing a word trick on you. There is a special name for words that sound exactly the same when you say them but are spelled differently and have different meanings. These words are *homonyms*. Try saying that.

Class: Homonyms.

Mrs. L.: Homonyms require us to know how to correctly spell words that may sound the same. One of the best things you can do to become familiar with homonyms is to...

Olivia: Read lots of books.

Billy: And look at the words carefully.

Mrs. L.: Exactly! Let's take a closer look at the other words in the sentences I have written on the chart. I think I may have made a few mistakes when I wrote some other homonyms. Let's save the "words that paint pictures" for another day and concentrate on the homonyms.

Abbey: You should fix the word *right*.

Mrs. L.: How about if I cross out w-r-i-t-e and write r-i-g-h-t above it. Now, does anyone see another homonym mistake in this same sentence?

Marc: Isn't the word *ear* in *hear*?

Bobby: Yes, *hear* is spelled h-e-a-r.

Mrs. L.: Since Granny and Grandpa didn't *hear* the phone ring, that means they are using their ears. This homonym has a wonderful clue for word detectives—*ear* is in the word *hear*—the kind of hear that you do with your ear. I'll fix this word. Is h-e-r-e a word?

Matthew: It means get over *here* right now.

Mrs. L.: Excellent word detecting! Some of the homonyms I have recorded on the chart are tricky ones. Look on the chart for a misspelled homonym and we'll fix it together.

(We continue going through the chart, finding and discussing homonyms.)

Mrs. L.: Homonyms are a fun challenge for word detectives. With experience, you'll look at homonyms when you write them and say, "That doesn't look right," and realize you used the incorrect homonym. Let's start practicing right now. Who can find another misspelled homonym?

It takes us two mini-lessons to find and change the incorrect homonyms on our chart of sentences. After the mini-lessons, I hang our homonym chart near the writing center for reference during writing time. It is helpful to see the correct usage of particular homonyms. By comparing the meanings of the crossed out and correct homonyms used in a sample sentence containing the word they are writing, students can figure out which word is the correct one for their sentence. As new homonyms arise, we discuss the meanings and spellings of each. Occasionally we add a third meaning to an already discussed homonym such as *right*—"I use my right hand to write."

Book Celebrations: Activities to Extend Learning

Sincerely, Arthur

Have your students proofread a letter from Arthur to the "Treat Timer" company explaining his problems based on the story *Arthur's TV Trouble* by Marc Brown. Students should cross out incorrect homonyms and write the correct homonym above each misspelled word. You may choose to copy page 149 on an overhead transparency, make individual copies for your students, or copy it on your board for a whole group lesson on homonyms. The incorrect homonyms have been underlined in the sample letter which follows but should not be underlined when the letter is shown to students!

<u>Deer</u> Makers of the Treat Timer,

   I am <u>righting</u> to tell you of my problem with your product. After counting my birthday money, and working <u>too</u> raise the rest of the money, I bought <u>won</u> of your treat timers <u>four</u> my dog, Pal. It took five <u>hole</u> hours to put it together! When I finally put the Treat Timer in front of Pal, it began flashing and clicking so Pal ran for cover. I guess my mother was <u>write</u> when she said Pal prefers getting treats from me, <u>knot</u> a machine.
   <u>Sew</u> that other pet owning kids like me do not scare their dogs with a Treat Timer, skip the lights and sounds so that dogs do not fear for <u>there</u> lives when trying to grab a treat. Oh, and try to find a way for the treats to land on the ground, not shoot across the room like rockets, <u>two</u>.

                Sincerely,
                Arthur
                An Unhappy Treat Timer Customer

Proofreader's Name: Rachel   Date: Sept 29

Dear Makers of the Treat Timer,

    I am ~~fighting~~ writing to tell you of my problem with your product. After counting my birthday money, and working ~~too~~ to raise the rest of the money, I bought ~~won~~ one of your treat timers ~~four~~ for my dog, Pal. It took five ~~hole~~ whole hours to put it together! When I finally put the Treat Timer in front of Pal, it began flashing and clicking so Pal ran for cover. I guess my mother was ~~write~~ right when she said Pal prefers getting treats from me, ~~knot~~ not a machine.

    ~~Sew~~ So that other pet owning kids like me do not scare their dogs with a treat timer, skip the lights and sounds so that dogs do not fear for ~~there~~ their lives when trying to grab a treat. Oh, and try to find a way for the treats to land on the ground, not shoot across the room like rockets, ~~two~~ too.

                   Sincerely,
                     Arthur
                     An Unhappy Treat Timer Customer

Student-corrected Arthur letter

Same Meaning, Different Words

    Reuse the favorite sentences chart from this lesson to explore synonyms. Define synonyms as different words that have nearly the same meaning, such as *big* and *large*, for example. Explain how synonyms are used to provide variety when writing the same tired or frequently used words (such as *said* and *nice*). Circle selected words from the sentences already copied on the chart. Suggestions for words to use for synonym practice are: *shouted, creaked, start, snuggly, cuddled, little, asked, said, ran* and *sweet*. Read each sentence aloud and have students think of a word that means about the same thing as the circled word. Read the sentences again using the synonyms, and then discuss which word sounds better.

Homonym & Synonym Challenge

For those students who always need an extra challenge, pass out copies of page 150 to complete. Students are to write a one-word synonym, homonym, and antonym for each word given (see the sample below from the reproducible page). Students may wish to work in pairs to complete this tricky assignment.

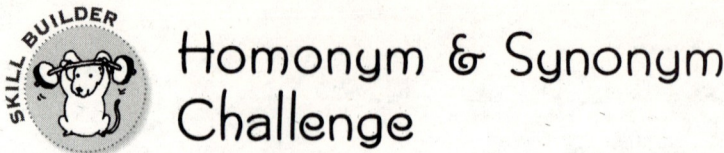

A Noun Pizza

GOAL To identify a noun as a person, place, or thing

As students develop their word power skills, their excitement about language grows. They love discovering the rules that govern our language and practicing the decoding strategies they've learned. Once I've covered a variety of word power skills and kindled their curiosity about language, I like to introduce the idea of parts of speech, the concept that types of words are grouped together and have a special name. While we worked with nouns and verbs when we explored word endings, I didn't use their grammatical names. But now kids are ready to learn about this important aspect of our language, and they love being able to categorize words based on their function.

I start our exploration of parts of speech with nouns. I begin the following mini-lesson on nouns by reading aloud Pete's a Pizza by William Steig (1998). The story is based upon a game William Steig used to play with his youngest daughter when she needed a little cheering up. He simply placed her on a table and turned her into a pizza! In the book, the pizza-making process that turns Pete into a pretend pizza elicits many giggles and gets kids ready to build their own pretend pizza out of nouns.

William Steig used items around the house to make his pizza—talcum powder for flour, water for oil, and pieces of paper for cheese. The students and I construct our pizza using items from the classroom, words, and our imaginations in this mini-lesson that helps students identify nouns as people, places, and things. Prior to the lesson, parent volunteers help to cut out various construction paper shapes to help us build our noun pizza. On another day, at the students' request, we extend the lesson by making real pizzas of our own—with things like pepperoni, cheese, and sauce!

Pete's a Pizza by William Steig ▶

Mrs. L.: You know, I just love the story *Pete's a Pizza* by William Steig.

Abbey: Is it one of your new favorite books?

Mrs. L.: Absolutely—I knew the first time I read it, that it would be a favorite. But I've always enjoyed William Steig's books and the dust jacket says this book is his 28th book for children! I think 28 books is an amazing accomplishment!

Bobby: *Pete's a Pizza* sounds like "Piece of Pizza."

Mrs. L.: I wonder if this is the reason William Steig chose the name "Pete".... It does go well with the word "pizza."

Bobby: I wish my dad would turn me into a pizza.

Mrs. L.: Well, how about if we make a pizza of our own today?

Anna: One to eat? For real?

Mrs. L.: Well, I thought we'd top it with some special words.

Jonathan: What?

Mrs. L.: I would like to make a word pizza!

Bobby: I knew it! Is that why you have a pizza crust drawn on the board?

Anna: Can we make a real pizza sometime?

Mrs. L.: I think that could be arranged. But today we're going to make a word pizza.

Jonathan: How do we make a word pizza?

Mrs. L.: We start by deciding what we want to have on our pizza. I think I'm in the mood for a noun pizza.

Stephanie: What do you mean, a noun pizza?

Mrs. L.: This pizza is going to be filled with all different kinds of things. You see, *noun* is the name we give to words that are people, places, or things. So your pizza can have people, places, or things on it.

Billy: I don't want people on my pizza!

Chris: I don't want places on my pizza.

Marc: I don't want things on my pizza—I want pepperoni!

John: Me, too.

Mrs. L.: Well, that's fine because *pepperoni* is a noun.

John: Good. I'd like double pepperoni.

Mrs. L.: Sorry, *double* can't be on a noun pizza.

Stephanie: Why not?

Mrs. L.: *Double* is not a person, place, or thing, so it's not a noun. Okay, I cut out some circles of paper. Since I wasn't sure what kinds of things you would want on our pizza, I cut out all different colors. Would you like red for pepperoni?

Class: Yes.

Mrs. L.: I'll write *pepperoni* on this red circle. Anna, would you please add it to our pizza crust?

Anna: Hey, you have to put tomato sauce on first.

Mrs. L.: Uh-oh. We can have *sauce* because it's a thing and a noun is a...

Class: Person, place, or thing.

Katie: What kind of sauce is it if it isn't tomato?

Mrs. L.: You'll just have to use your imagination on this word pizza. Remember, describing words are not nouns.

David: And this is a noun pizza!

Mrs. L.: Exactly! Would you like to use red paper for the sauce also?

Molly: Sure. I can spell sauce for you: s-o-s.

Mrs. L.: Good sound-spelling.

Stephanie: That doesn't look right.

Mrs. L.: I'll put book-spelling underneath it so that you can see how silly our language can be. What's next?

Greg: Extra cheese.

Mrs. L.: You can have *cheese* because that's a thing too. But *extra* is a word that describes the cheese, and—

Rachel: We're only putting nouns on our pizza today.

Greg: Oops!

Mrs. L.: Yellow paper for cheese?

Carrie: Yes—c-h-e-e-s.

Marc: It needs an *e* at the end—cheese has two vowels and a Bossy E.

Mrs. L.: Definitely a long *e*! Nice spelling.

Mathew: My brother likes black olives on his pizza and I sort of like them.

Mrs. L.: We can only put one of those words on our noun pizza. *Black* or *olives*—which word is a thing?

Class: Olives.

Mrs. L.: Great. I'll write it on black paper: *o-l-i-v-e-s*.

Allisa: That word breaks the Bossy E rule.

Mrs. L.: It sure does. So far we have *pepperoni*, *sauce*, *cheese*, and *olives* on our pizza. Anything else?

Alex: I love mushrooms. We could put mushrooms on it—they are things.

Abbey: We could label the crust because it's a thing too.

Mrs. L.: Good idea. I'll just write *crust* on the edge of the pizza. *C-r-u-s-t*.

Bobby: Finally, a word that looks like it should!

Mrs. L.: I think our noun pizza looks delicious. Let's reread *Pete's a Pizza* for fun. I'd like you to listen for more nouns. I think you are experts on finding things that are nouns. Listen to the story and tell me if you hear any other people or places or things that are nouns and I'll write them around our pizza. After I read each page, I'll stop so we can discuss the nouns in *Pete's a Pizza*. Here's the first page.

> Pete's in a bad mood. Just when he's supposed to play ball with the guys, it decides to rain.

John: Pete is a person.

Mrs. L.: Pete is a noun. I'll write it on the board.

Jonathan: What about *ball*? He wanted to play ball. That's a thing.

Mrs. L.:	Yes, it is.
Sara:	*Guys* and *rain* are people and things.
Mrs. L.:	Great word detecting! Pages 2 and 3 are pictures, so let's go on to page 4.

> Pete's father can't help noticing how miserable his son is.

Anna:	*Pete's father* is a noun.
Mrs. L.:	One of these is a noun, and the other is a word that tells us whose father "can't help noticing how miserable his son is."
Carrie:	A father is a person, so *father* is the noun.
Mrs. L.:	Great job!
Chris:	*Son* is a thing.
Mrs. L.:	There are two kinds of sons and they are homonyms. If you are a boy, you are a son—a special kind of person.
Matthew:	The sun in the sky is a thing. So it's a noun.
Mrs. L.:	Good thinking—both s-o-n and s-u-n are nouns. Which one did William Steig use on this page?
Allisa:	The "boy" kind
Mrs. L.:	Right! Let's try pages 6 and 7.

> So he sets him down on the kitchen table and starts kneading the dough…

Tommy:	*Kitchen table* is a thing.
Mrs. L.:	Which of these words is the actual thing you can touch? *Kitchen* or *table*?
Katie:	Just *table* is the thing.
Marc:	I think *dough* is a noun—it's a thing.
Mrs. L.:	These all sound like things to me! I'll read the next few pages.

> …and stretching it this way and that. Now the dough gets whirled and twirled up in the air.

Stephanie:	Is *air* a thing? You can't touch it.
Mrs. L.:	I think since we know it's there, we can call *air* a thing, so *air* is a noun. Try these sentences.

> Next, some oil is generously applied. (It's really water.)
> Then comes some flour. (It's really talcum powder.)

Sara:	*Oil* and *water* are things.
Carrie:	*Flour* is a thing.
Billy:	So is *baby powder*.
David:	I think *powder* is the noun.
Mrs. L.:	Yes, *talcum* is the same as *baby powder*. These words describe the kind of powder. Let's name a few more nouns.

We continue reading a few more pages and elicit the words *tomatoes, checkers, mother, paper, cheese, Petey, stuff, Pizza-Makers, oven, sun,* and *friends* as "Pete's Pizza Nouns." I end by inviting the students to make a noun pizza of their very own.

Book Celebrations:
Activities to Extend Learning

Personal Noun Pizzas

The pizzas we make are almost like the personal pizzas served at that famous pizza place, except ours are topped with nouns and a sprinkling of adjectives. Using scrap paper found in our art center scrap box, students make pizzas filled with their favorite pizza nouns. Students begin by cutting out a paper "crust" upon which they put any noun "toppings" they would like. Since most students still crave extra cheese and double pepperoni, I have them write these "describing words" on white paper to be differentiated from the nouns. We discuss these describing words and label them as "adjectives." I join in on the fun by making my favorite pizza, with extra cheese, thin crust, homemade sauce, greasy pepperoni, and green olives!

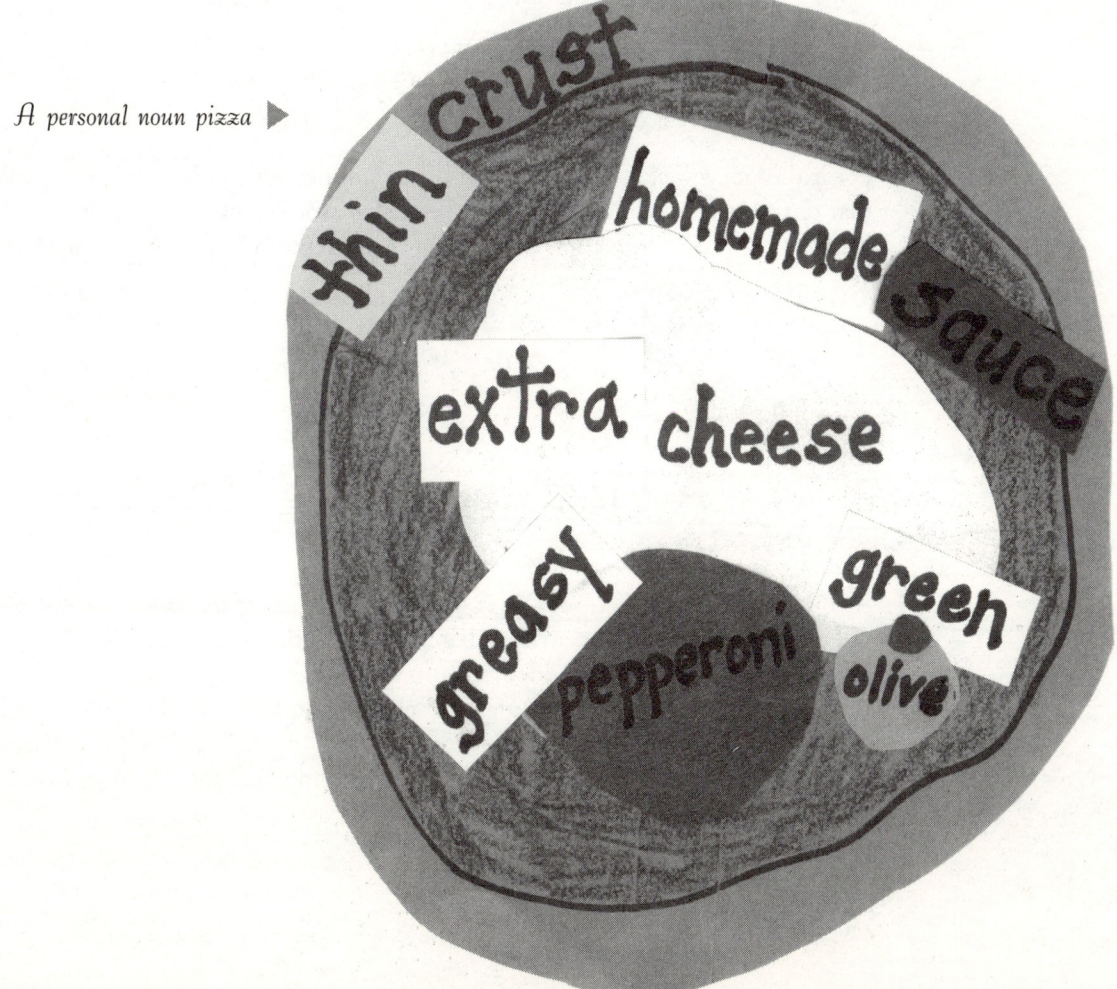

A personal noun pizza ▶

English Muffin Pizza

For a quick and easy cooking lesson that complements the book *Pete's a Pizza*, we make individual pizzas using English muffins as crust. Parents donate toppings for our pizza-building project; they bring in sauce, cheese, pepperoni, and assorted other toppings to share*. After the students construct their pizza masterpieces, a parent volunteer cooks and delivers them to the students' tables while I read a story to the class. (If available, a microwave oven is a quick, convenient way to heat pizzas.) Fun stories to complement a pizza party are *Curious George and the Pizza* by Maragret Rey (1985) and *How Pizza Came to Queens* by Dayal Kaur Khalsa (1995).

While eating our pizza, we list verbs that describe how we are eating the hot, delicious pizza.

Mrs. L.	devours	pizza.
Sara	munches	pizza.
John	chows on	pizza.
Carrie	nibbles	pizza.
Bobby	gobbles	pizza.
Rachel	crunches	pizza.
Katie	bites big bites of	pizza.

For extra fun as well as to expand our list of "munching words," we make a rule that once a person names a particular verb, that word cannot be used again. This list becomes our introduction to verbs, or "action words," in a future mini-lesson.

A Pizza the Size of the Sun

A collection of zany poetry is found in *A Pizza the Size of the Sun* by Jack Prelutsky (1996). Chart the cover poem and share it along with slices of English Muffin Pizzas (see above) for some added pizza fun. Children "ooh and aahh" while reading of oceans of sauce, mountains of cheese, and acres of pepperoni on this "wonderful pizza the size of the sun." Surprisingly, my pizza lovers did not seem too disappointed to learn that it will take a year and a half for this pizza to bake!

---

* Be sure to check with parents about any possible food allergies your students might have.

School House Rock

Need a refresher course on nouns, verbs, and adjectives? Check out *Grammar Rock*, a School House Rock! Video, presented by Disney's Buena Vista Home Video (1995), for a review of words such as adjectives, verbs, nouns, adverbs, prepositions, and conjunctions. The catchy tunes that accompany the silly cartoons make learning the rules of grammar fun and easy. Learn about nouns by singing "Any person you can know, any place that you can go, and any thing that you can show, you know they're nouns…" Action words are remembered with the words "Verbs, you're what's happening: to be, to see, to feel, to live…" And pronouns are important because "saying all those nouns can really wear you down." Frames that announce each upcoming segment make fast-forwarding to the grammar subject of your choice quick and easy.

Best Friends— Never Spit on Your Shoes…

A quick assessment activity for nouns and verbs begins with some simple sentences like those listed below from the books *Never Spit on Your Shoes* by Denys Cazet and *Best Friends* by Steven Kellogg. Copy the sentences on an overhead transparency or on the board for an overall class assessment of nouns and verbs. Have students copy the nouns and verbs on individual sheets of paper as you read the sentences aloud. For an added challenge, omit a noun or verb from a sentence and have students fill in an appropriate word.

Find the action words in the following sentences from *Best Friends*.

1. At school we <u>pushed</u> our desks together.
2. And we <u>played</u> on the same team.
3. At lunch we <u>shared</u> our chocolate milk.
4. After school we <u>pretended</u> that we <u>rode</u> Golden Silverwind.

Find the nouns in the following sentences from *Never Spit on Your Shoes*.

1. <u>Arnie</u> slammed the screen <u>door</u> and flopped into a <u>chair</u>.
2. "<u>Milk!</u>" he gasped.
3. Arnie's <u>mother</u> poured cold <u>milk</u> into a <u>glass</u>.
4. He reached into his <u>backpack</u> and pulled out a <u>piece</u> of <u>paper</u>.

Review With Yoko

GOAL To review word-power skills

Yoko is a delightful story by Rosemary Wells that explores a typical school day with all its disappointments and excitements through a little girl named Yoko. Yoko, with her lunch box full of sushi wrapped in a willow-covered cooler, smiles until lunchtime, when all the others make fun of her unusual lunch. Another book with many uses—from exploring individual differences and discussing the benefits of accepting others, to relating to another person's feelings and being a friend—Yoko has a place in every primary classroom.

Although the following review mini-lesson would work with any book on your classroom bookshelf, I chose Yoko for several reasons. I felt the short, one-to-three sentences of text per page would be ideal for the review lesson I was imagining. With closer examination, I found all the word power skills I wanted to assess represented in this book. And best of all, my students loved Yoko.

I marked the pages of Yoko with Post-It Notes, on which I wrote the skill I planned to review with that page. Page one, for example, has two -ed words, two l-blend words, two silent e words, one Rainbow Rule word, five short-vowel words and four long-vowel words. I decided to review l-blends using this page and marked the Post-It Note with this skill. I made copies of Reviewing With Yoko (pages 151–152) and collected individual lap boards for recording. After reading and discussing Yoko for fun during Read Aloud, I reread it page by page on another day. This time, as the students listened and recorded particular words given as clues, I assessed their understanding of word power skills.

◄ <u>Yoko</u>
by Rosemary Wells

MANAGEMENT TIP

Although there are many possibilities for reviewing different kinds of words on each page, I found that my first graders had a difficult time listening for more than one kind of word at a time. So I had them focus on one skill per page: "Listen for a compound word as I read this page."

Mrs. L.:	Now it's time to put your word power skills to the test! While I reread *Yoko* by Rosemary Wells, I would like you to write some special words on a Reviewing with *Yoko* recording sheet.
Billy:	You mean words with an ending?
Mrs. L.:	Yes, sometimes you'll look for a word with an ending, sometimes you'll look for a word that starts with a certain blend—
Sara:	Or a vowel sound.
Mrs. L.:	Exactly. What other special words have we talked about in our word power mini-lessons?
Chris:	Cinnamons.
Sara:	You mean synonyms.
Allisa:	Rhyming words.
Matthew:	Beats in words—
Tommy:	Syllables.
John:	Compound words.
Molly:	Vowels.
Alex:	Rainbow Rule words.
Marc:	Bossy E words.
Mrs. L.:	Can you think of any other kinds of words?
Carrie:	And words that sound the same but have different spellings.
Mrs. L.:	Homonyms. I'm impressed by your good memories! *Yoko* is going to help us review these word detective skills. I'll read each page, asking you to find a particular kind of word. I may say, "Listen for a word that ends with *-ed*." Then you should write an *-ed* word in the appropriate space on your paper.
Tommy:	What if I can't spell it?
Mrs. L.:	I know you'll be able to sound-spell any word I read.
Matthew:	We can sound-spell any word in the world!
Mrs. L.:	I like your confidence! Let's give *Yoko* a try.

(With the students' help, I distribute "Reviewing With *Yoko*" recording sheets and lap boards.)

Mrs. L.:	On page one, please listen for a word that begins with an *l*-blend. Write this word and circle the beginning blend.

> "What would you like for lunch today, my little cherry blossom?" asked Yoko's mother. "All my favorite things, please," answered Yoko.

(After giving students time to sound-spell the word(s) individually, we take time to discuss each word.)

Sara:	I heard two words on that page so I wrote them both down.
Mrs. L.:	I wondered why you were doing so much writing! What two words did you write?
Sara:	*Please* and *blossom*.
Mrs. L.:	Excellent word detecting. Tell me about the *l*-blends.
Sara:	*Please* has *pl* and *blossom* has *bl*.
Mrs. L.:	Great! Smile if you put a certain silent letter on the end of *please*.
Cassie:	You mean Bossy E.
Mrs. L.:	Right. Go ahead an add a Bossy E to *please* if you haven't already.
Allisa:	I thought this word was a Rainbow Word.
Mrs. L.:	Guess what! *Please* follows both of the long vowel rules. Tell me the letter that does the talking in *please*, please!
Carrie:	E. A walks, I think.
Mrs. L.:	Right again! Let's try page two. Listen for a word that ends in *-ed*. I'll give you a hint, there will be more than one word on this page that ends in *-ed*. Copy at least one of the words you hear, please.

> Yoko's mother spread steamed rice on a bamboo mat. She rolled up a secret treasure inside each piece. Then she packed it all in a willow-covered cooler.

Molly:	I heard three words with *-ed*.
Stephanie:	I heard four!
Mrs. L.:	*-ed* is a well-used ending, isn't it? What words did you hear?
Molly:	*Packed, rolled,* and *steamed*.
Stephanie:	*Willow-covered.* But I only wrote *covered*.
Mrs. L.:	That's fine. I'll give you a chance to circle the *-ed* endings on these words or copy another *-ed* word that you may have missed.
Chris:	Do we have to copy all four?
Mrs. L.:	No, but how about two for sure.

On the next page, please find a word that means more than one—with an *-s* or *-es* ending—and circle the ending.

> Yoko said hello to all her friends.
> Everyone in Mrs. Jenkins's class sang the Good Morning Song.

Billy:	I found it—*friends*.
Mrs. L.:	Great detecting! "Yoko said hello to all her friends."

Molly:	I heard another one—*class*.
Alex:	No, it's just one *class*. More than one would be *classes*. That *s* is part of the word.
Mrs. L.:	Right. Don't let these words trick you! Listen for another *-s* or *-es* word on the next page, too.

> At noon Mrs. Jenkins rang the lunch bell.
> "Lunch boxes out and open, please, boys and girls!" said Mrs. Jenkins.

Katie:	I found two—*boys* and *girls*.
Mrs. L.:	Did you add *-s* or *-es*?
Class:	*-s*.
Mrs. L.:	Great!
Rachel:	There's another one too—*boxes*. That has *-es*.
Mrs. L.:	Excellent detecting! *B-o-x-e-s*. Find a compound word on the next page, please.

> Timothy unwrapped a peanut butter and honey sandwich. Valerie had cream cheese and jelly. Fritz had a meatball grinder. Tulip had Swiss cheese on rye.

Greg:	It's *meatball*—balls of meat!
Mrs. L.:	Nice work!
Carrie:	What about *peanut*? I know it's not a nut made out of a pea, but it is two words inside a big word.
Mrs. L.:	I'd say we could count *peanut* as a compound word even though the meaning of the two words doesn't seem to be related. I'm going to read this page again. This time, find a word that has a long *e* sound.

(I read the page again.)

Greg:	I heard lots. I only had time to copy down *peanut* and *honey*.
Sara:	I wrote down *cream*.
Olivia:	And *cheese*.
Mrs. L.:	You could also copy *meatball* again on your long *e* list, couldn't you. Look at your list of long *e* words and put a star next to the ones you think follow the Rainbow Rule.
Billy:	I think *meatball* is a rainbow word.
Mrs. L.:	What two vowels walk together?
Class:	*E* and *a*.
Mrs. L.:	Great. If you don't have *m-e-a-t* at the beginning of *meatball*, you can change it now. Any other rainbow words?
Anna:	Yes! *Cream* and *cheese*.
Mrs. L.:	Right. One of those words is a rainbow word and a Bossy E word.
Marc:	*Cheese* is the Bossy E word.
Mrs. L.:	*Cream* has the same two vowels walking as *meatball*.
Jonathan:	*C-r-e-a-m*. That's an *r*-blend word too.

Mrs. L.:	Good eyes. Go ahead and copy *cream* under blends also. I'll read the next page slowly so you can listen for a word that has four beats. Hazel had egg salad on pumpernickel. Doris had squeeze cheese on white, and the Franks had franks and beans.
Class:	*Pum-per-nick-el!*
Mrs. L.:	Excellent! That's a challenging word to spell. Sound it out by syllables, and it will be easier. On the next page, please find a word that rhymes with *twice*.

After reading and discussing pages until we have reviewed most of our word detective skills, I finish reading *Yoko* just for fun. The students keep their recording sheets close at hand and as the day progresses, we stop to add words to our list of special words. During Read Aloud, we add *Noisy Nora's* mon-u-men-tal crash to our list of words with four beats (Wells, 1973). During math, we include *fractions* to our list of *r-blend* words. This ongoing activity helps students look at words with a critical eye as they continue their journey as readers.

Reviewing with *Yoko*

Book Celebrations: Activities to Extend Learning

Words of the Week

To help students focus on and review a particular skill, we make Words of the Week booklets. To do this, staple ten sheets of lined paper inside a construction paper cover. On the first day of each week, I identify the words to be reviewed—one week we'll review compound words, another short vowels, and so on. I list these words on the board as they come up throughout the day. At some point, I give the students five to ten minutes to copy them into their books, highlighting the featured skill—coloring rainbow vowels with crayons, tracing over the *-ed* endings with red marker, and so on. This activity also provides a recording space for any new skills that are introduced. These Words of the Week can also be included in Word Power Notebooks, although additional pages may need to be added for this review!

Rachel works on initial consonant blends. ▶

Word Power Assessment: Assessing With Chrysanthemum

On another day, we go through the review process again using the book *Chrysanthemum* by Kevin Henkes, beginning with recording *Chrysanthemum* as a word with four syllables. The difference on this day is that the review activity is now an assessment tool that I call "Assessing with *Chrysanthemum*." I ask students to record words as they did in our mini-lesson, without pausing to discuss each word when I read it. When finished, I collect the recording sheets and evaluate the students' understanding of the skills covered. This activity also allows me to see how their sound-spelling is progressing. I check to see if a word that is included as a rainbow word is written with two vowels walking together. This activity is a fun way to assess skills and reread a favorite book at the same time. (See the Student Snapshot below for more ideas on how to assess with this book.)

Sara, Grade 1

WORKING WITH A FLUENT READER

Sara walked through the door of my classroom on the first day of school as a fluent reader. A true reading enthusiast, she has identified authors and books as her favorites and is always anxious for a challenging new book or activity. One day, as an independent activity, I gave Sara a copy of the book *Chrysanthemum* by Kevin Henkes, one of this young reader's favorite authors. I asked Sara to read the book and mark with Post-It Notes some of the pages containing special words, as I had done with *Yoko*. After reviewing her ideas, I then helped her select a few of the pages she had marked that included examples of various word study skills for her classmates to explore as an independent activity.

To help students more easily identify the pages being discussed, we numbered them in pencil, beginning with the first page of text.

Mrs. L.:	Let's take a look at some of the special words you discovered in the book *Chrysanthemum*.
Sara:	I found lots of good words.
Mrs. L.:	Great! Let's try to find a few favorite special words.
Sara:	Should they be tricky ones?
Mrs. L.:	They should be challenging and help your classmates practice as many different kinds of words as possible.
Sara:	My favorite page is the one with the names of everyone in Chrysanthemum's class.
Mrs. L.:	It looks like many of the names are consonant-vowel-consonant words.
Sara:	I think there's a name for every vowel sound—at least the short ones.
Mrs. L.:	Let's make sure. Is there a name for short *a*?
Sara:	*Al* and *Pat. Max*, too. The *a* in *Sam* sounds different.
Mrs. L.:	That's because the *m* changes the sound of the *a* like the letter *r* in the word *car*. The vowels in these words are controlled by *m* and *r*. Looks like there are plenty of other short *a* words to choose from. What about short *e*?
Sara:	*Ken*.
Mrs. L.:	I see another one.
Sara:	Oh, *Les*.
Mrs. L.:	What about *Eve*?
Sara:	Bossy E makes it a long *e*.
Mrs. L.:	Any short *i* words?
Sara:	*Bill* and *Victoria*.
Mrs. L.:	What about *Lois* and *Rita*? I see an *i* in these words too.
Sara:	*Lois* has a long *o*, but I guess the *i* is short. *Rita* sounds like long *e*.
Mrs. L.:	There are several short *i* names to choose from without *Lois* and *Rita* anyway.
Sara:	*Don* and *Tom* have short *o*; *Jo* and *Lois* have long *o*.
Mrs. L.:	Excellent job. The only vowel left is *u*.
Sara:	*Mrs. Chud* has short *u*. So does *Chrysanthemum*. *Sue* is long.
Mrs. L.:	I agree. Let's use one of my big Post-It Notes to mark this page with the sentence "Find names with short vowels *a, e, i, o,* and *u*." Nice printing, Sara. Let's look for another page with different words.
Sara:	How about page 14? It has -ed words—*walked* and *dragged*.
Mrs. L.:	Yes, it does. Here's a Post-It Note for you to write "Find an -ed word."
Sara:	They can choose which -ed word to write. Next, I'll use page 16. In the picture it says, "Words We Know." I'll write, "Find a rainbow word and a Bossy E word on the chalkboard." *Tail* and *cheese* are the words to find.
Mrs. L.:	I like that idea. Any others?

Sara: I like the "hugs and kisses and Parcheesi" on page 19. I'll have them find words with -s and -es.

Mrs. L.: That's one of my favorite pages too. I like the way the dad is reading a book about Chrysanthemum's problem while he hugs her. Did you find any pages with compound words?

Sara: I'll look. Page 25 has *grandmother*.

Mrs. L.: Perfect! Why don't you write, "Find a compound word" on the Post-It Note. You've found words with endings, short and long vowels, and compound words.

Sara: How about a rhyming word page? But this isn't a rhyming word book.

Mrs. L.: Look for one of your favorite pages—I have an idea for rhyming words.

Sara: How about page 27 where Chrysanthemum blushed and bloomed?

Mrs. L.: Perfect! Now think of a word that rhymes with *blushed* or *bloomed*.

Sara: *Zoomed* rhymes with *bloomed*.

Mrs. L.: So on the Post-It Note write, "Find a word that rhymes with *zoomed*."

Sara: That's a good one!

Mrs. L.: I've found a page with an *l-blend* and an *r-blend*. It's page 13.

Sara: *Pleasant* and *dream* are the words with blends. I'll write "Find an *l-blend* word and an *r-blend* word."

Mrs. L.: You've come up with some excellent words for your friends to explore. You are definitely an expert on special words. Tomorrow you can explain this activity to the rest of the class.

Sara's knowledge of word skills impressed me, and although her thorough understanding of words from vowel sounds to endings was more advanced than the other students', she served as an excellent model and a helpful adviser.

To encourage others to look more closely at words, before silent reading on another day, I pass out two small Post-It Notes to each student. I ask them to find and mark two pages, each with a different kind of special word, in the book they've chosen for this quiet reading time. We take a few minutes to share these words and the class continues to sharpen word power skills.

Chrysanthemum
by Kevin Henkes ▶

Proofreader's Name _____ Date _____

Deer Makers of the Treat Timer,

   I am righting to tell you of my problem with your product. After counting my birthday money, and working too raise the rest of the money, I bought won of your treat timers four my dog, Pal. It took five hole hours to put it together! When I finally put the Treat Timer in front of Pal, it began flashing and clicking so Pal ran for cover. I guess my mother was write when she said Pal prefers getting treats from me, knot a machine.

   Sew that other pet owning kids like me do not scare their dogs with a treat timer, skip the lights and sounds so that dogs do not fear for there lives when trying to grab a treat. Oh, and try to find a way for the treats to land on the ground, not shoot across the room like rockets, two.

                        Sincerely,

                        Arthur

                        An Unhappy Treat Timer Customer

Name _____ Date _____

Word Power Challenge

Read each word below. Fill in the chart to include a word that means the same (synonym), a word that sounds the same (homonym), and a word that is the opposite (antonym) of each given word.

Word	Synonym	Homonym	Antonym
in	inside	inn	out
ate			
groan			
hear			
need			
night			
real			
steal			
threw			
weak			

Bonus! Think of another word that has a synonym, homonym, and antonym. Add this word to the chart along with its synonym, homonym, and antonym.

Name _____ Date _____

Review With Yoko

Rhyming Words

1. ....
2. ....
3. ....
4. ....

Compound Words

1. ....
2. ....
3. ....
4. ....

-ed Words

1. ....
2. ....
3. ....
4. ....

-s or -es Words

1. ....
2. ....
3. ....
4. ....

-ing Words

1. ....
2. ....
3. ....
4. ....

Words with Blends

1. ....
2. ....
3. ....
4. ....

Name _____ Date _____

Rainbow Words

1. ....
2. ....
3. ....
4. ....

Bossy E Words

1. ....
2. ....
3. ....
4. ....

Short Vowel Words

1. ....
2. ....
3. ....
4. ....

3-Syllable Words

1. ....
2. ....
3. ....
4. ....

4-Syllable Words

1. ....
2. ....
3. ....
4. ....

Homonyms

1. ....
2. ....

Synonyms

1. ....
2. ....

Books to Use: Books for Reviewing Word Power Skills

The Art Lesson by Tomie dePaola (G.P. Putnam's Sons, 1989)

Arthur's Halloween by Marc Brown (Little, Brown and Company, 1982)

Arthur's TV Trouble by Marc Brown (Little, Brown and Company, 1995)

Chrysanthemum by Kevin Henkes (Greenwillow Books, 1991)

The Day the Goose Got Loose by Reeve Lindbergh (Dial Books for Young Readers, 1990)

Falling Up by Shel Silverstein (HarperCollins, 1996)

In the Night Kitchen by Maurice Sendak (Harper & Row Publishers, 1970)

Lyle Finds His Mother by Bernard Waber (Houghton Mifflin Company, 1974)

Mr. Putter and Tabby Pour the Tea by Cynthia Rylant (Harcourt Brace & Company, 1994)

Night Noises by Mem Fox (Harcourt Brace Jovanovich, Inc., 1989)

Noisy Nora by Rosemary Wells (Dial Books for Young Readers, 1973)

Rats on the Roof and Other Stories by James Marshall (Dial Books for Young Readers, 1991)

Tell Me Again About the Night I Was Born by Jamie Lee Curtis (HarperCollins, 1996)

Whatever Happened to the Dinosaurs? by Bernard Most (Harcourt Brace Jovanovich, Inc., 1984)

Where's My Teddy? by Jez Alborough (Candlewick Press, 1992)

The Wump World by Bill Peet (Houghton Mifflin Company, 1970)

Yoko by Rosemary Wells (Hyperion Books for Children, 1998)

APPENDIX

Book Lists

Comprehensive List of Books Used Throughout the Mini-Lessons

Alborough, Jez. *Where's My Teddy?*. Cambridge: Candlewick Press, 1992.

Aliki. *How a Book Is Made*. New York: Harper & Row Publishers, 1986.

Brown, Marc. *Arthur Babysits*. Boston: Little, Brown and Company, 1992.

———. *Arthur's Birthday*. Boston: Little, Brown and Company, 1989.

———. *Arthur's First Sleepover*. Boston: Little, Brown and Company, 1994.

———. *Arthur's Halloween*. Boston: Little, Brown and Company, 1982.

———. *Arthur's Thanksgiving*. Boston: Little, Brown and Company, 1983.

———. *Arthur's TV Trouble*. Boston: Little, Brown and Company, 1995.

———. *Arthur Writes a Story*. Boston: Little, Brown and Company, 1996.

Carle, Eric. *The Grouchy Ladybug*. New York: HarperCollins, 1977.

Cherry, Lynne. *Flute's Journey: The Life of a Wood Thrush*. New York: Harcourt Brace & Company, 1997.

Christelow, Eileen. *Five Little Monkeys Jumping on the Bed.* New York: Clarion Books, 1989.

———. *Five Little Monkeys Sitting in a Tree.* New York: Houghton Mifflin Company, 1991.

Curtis, Jamie Lee. *Tell Me Again About the Night I Was Born.* New York: HarperCollins, 1996.

Degan, Bruce. *Jamberry.* New York: HarperCollins, 1983.

dePaola, Tomie. *The Art Lesson.* New York: G.P. Putnam's Sons, 1989.

Egielski, Richard. *The Gingerbread Boy.* New York: HarperCollins, 1997.

Ehlert, Lois. *Eating the Alphabet: Fruits and Vegetables From A to Z.* New York: Harcourt Brace & Company, 1996.

———. *Feathers for Lunch.* New York: Harcourt Brace & Company, 1990.

———. *Fish Eyes: A Book You Can Count On.* New York: Harcourt Brace Jovanovich, 1992.

———. *Nuts to You.* New York: Harcourt Brace Jovanovich, 1993.

———. *Planting a Rainbow.* New York: Harcourt Brace & Company, 1988.

———. *Snowballs.* New York: Harcourt Brace & Company, 1995.

Fox, Mem. *Night Noises.* Orlando: Harcourt Brace Jovanovich, 1989.

Henkes, Kevin. *Chrysanthemum.* New York: Greenwillow Books, 1991.

Hopkins, Lee Bennett. *Good Books, Good Times!* New York: HarperCollins, 1990.

James, Simon. *Dear Mr. Blueberry.* New York: Aladdin Paperbacks, 1991.

Johnson, Angela. *Julius.* New York: Orchard Books, 1993.

Kirk, David. *Miss Spider's Tea Party.* New York: Scholastic Press, 1997.

Lester, Helen. *The Wizard, the Fairy, and the Magic Chicken.* Boston: Houghton, Mifflin Company, 1983.

Lindbergh, Reeve. *The Day the Goose Got Loose.* New York: Dial Books for Young Readers, 1990.

Mahy, Margaret. *17 Kings and 42 Elephants.* New York: Dial Books for Young Readers, 1987.

Marshall, James. *Fox on the Job.* New York: Dial Books for Young Readers, 1988.

———. *Rats on the Roof and Other Stories.* New York: Dial Books for Young Readers, 1991.

Martin, Bill. *Brown Bear, Brown Bear, What Do You See?* New York: Harcourt Brace & Company, 1967.

Martin, Bill and John Archambault. *Chicka Chicka Boom Boom.* New York: Simon & Schuster, 1989.

Mayer, Mercer. *Me Too.* New York: Golden Books Publishing Company, Inc., 1997.

———. *There's Something in My Attic.* New York: Dial Books for Young Readers, 1988.

McCloskey, Robert. *Blueberries for Sal.* New York: Viking Press, 1976.

Merriam, Eve. *Blackberry Ink.* New York: William Morrow and Company, 1985.

Most, B. *Whatever Happened to the Dinosaurs?* Orlando: Harcourt Brace Jovanovich, 1984.

Munsch, Robert. *The Paper Bag Princess.* Toronto: Annick Press LTD, 1980.

Noble, Trina Hakes. *Jimmy's Boa and the Big Splash Birthday Bash.* New York: Dial Books for Young Readers, 1989.

Numeroff, Laura. *If You Give a Moose a Muffin.* New York: HarperCollins, 1991.

―――――. *If You Give a Mouse a Cookie.* New York: Harper & Row, 1985.

―――――. *If You Give a Pig a Pancake.* New York: HarperCollins, 1998.

Peet, Bill. *The Wump World.* Boston: Houghton Mifflin Company, 1970.

Pilkey, Dav. *Dragon Gets By.* New York: Orchard Books, 1991.

―――――. *'Twas the Night Before Thanksgiving.* New York: Orchard Books, 1990.

Plourde, Lynn. *Pigs in the Mud in the Middle of the Rud.* New York: The Blue Sky Press, 1997.

Polacco, Patricia. *Just Plain Fancy.* New York: Bantam Doubleday Dell Publishing Group. 1990.

―――――. *My Rotten Redheaded Older Brother.* New York: Simon & Schuster, 1994.

―――――. *Mrs. Katz and Tush.* New York: Bantam Books for Young Readers, 1992.

―――――. *Picnic at Mudsock Meadow.* New York: G.P. Putnam's Sons, 1992.

―――――. *Some Birthday.* New York: Simon and Schuster Books for Young Readers, 1991.

Prelutsky, Jack. *The New Kid on the Block.* New York: Greenwillow Books, 1984.

―――――. *Something Big Has Been Here.* New York: Greenwillow Books, 1990.

Pulver, Robin. *The Holiday Handwriting School.* New York: Macmillan Publishing Company, 1991.

Rankin, Laura. *The Handmade Alphabet.* New York: Dial Books, 1991.

Riley, Linnea. *Mouse Mess.* New York: The Blue Sky Press, 1997.

Rosenberg, Liz. *Monster Mama.* New York: Philomel Books, 1993.

Rylant, Cynthia. *The Bookshop Dog.* New York: The Blue Sky Press, 1996.

―――――. *Henry and Mudge and the Bedtime Thumps.* New York: Macmillan Publishing Company, 1991.

―――――. *Henry and Mudge in the Green Time.* New York: Bradbury Press, 1987.

―――――. *Henry and Mudge Take the Big Test.* New York: Bradbury Press, 1991.

―――――. *Henry and Mudge and the Wild Wind.* New York: Bradbury Press, 1993.

————. *Mr. Putter and Tabby Pour the Tea*. New York: Harcourt Brace & Company, 1994.

————. *Tulip Sees America*. New York: Blue Sky Press, 1998.

Schwartz, Harriet Berg. *Backstage with Clawdio*. New York: Alfred A. Knopf, Inc., 1993.

Sendak, Maurice. *In the Night Kitchen*. New York: Harper & Row Publishers, 1970.

Seuss, Dr. *There's a Wocket in My Pocket*. New York: Random House, Inc., 1974.

Silverstein, Shel. *Falling Up*. New York: HarperCollins, 1996.

————. *Where the Sidewalk Ends*. New York: Harper and Row, 1974.

Steig, William. *The Amazing Bone*. New York: Farrar Straus Giroux., 1976.

————. *Sylvester and the Magic Pebble*. New York: Simon & Schuster, Inc., 1969.

Tolhurst, Marilyn. *Somebody and the Three Blairs*. New York: Orchard Books, 1990.

Van Allsburg, Chris. *Jumanji*. Boston: Houghton Mifflin Company, 1981.

————. *Just a Dream*. Boston: Houghton Mifflin Company, 1990.

Waber, Bernard. *Lyle Finds His Mother*. Boston: Houghton Mifflin Company, 1974.

Wells, Rosemary. *Fritz and the Mess Fairy*. New York: Dial Books for Young Readers, 1991.

————. *Max's Dragon Shirt*. New York: Dial Books for Young Readers, 1991.

————. *Noisy Nora*. New York: Dial Books for Young Readers, 1997.

————. *Yoko*. New York: Hyperion Books for Children, 1998.

Williams, Sherley Anne. *Working Cotton*. New York: Harcourt Brace & Company, 1992.

Williams, Vera. *A Chair for My Mother*. New York: Greenwillow Books, 1982.

Yolen, Jane. *Owl Moon*. New York: The Putnam Publishing Group, 1987.

Young, Ed. *Seven Blind Mice*. New York: Philomel Books, 1992.

References

Lunsford, Susan. *Literature Based Mini-Lessons to Teach Writing*. New York: Scholastic Professional Books, 1998.

Reading Yellow Pages for Students and Teachers. Nashville, TN: Incentive Publications, Inc., 1988.

The Favorite Books Box

More Recommended Books for Teaching Word Skills

More Books to Use for Rhyming Words:

Lewis, J. Patrick. *A Hippopotamusn't*. New York: Dial Books for Young Readers, 1990.

Moss, Lloyd. *Zin! Zin! Zin! a Violin*. New York: Scholastic Inc., 1995.

Prelutsky, Jack. *Poems of A. Nonny Mouse*. New York: Alfred A. Knopf, 1989.

——————. *The Random House Book of Poetry for Children*. New York: Random House, 1983.

——————. *Zoo Doings*. New York: Greenwillow Books, 1983.

Seuss, Dr. *Mr. Brown Can Moo Can You? Dr. Seuss's Book of Wonderful Noises*. New York: Random House, Inc., 1970.

Spinelli, Eileen. *When Mama Comes Home Tonight*. New York: Simon & Schuster, 1998.

More Books for Words With Happy Endings:

Carle, Eric. *The Very Hungry Caterpillar*. New York: Philomel Books, 1969.

Martin, Bill and John Archambault. *Knots on a Counting Rope*. New York: Henry Holt and Company, Inc., 1967

Mayer, Mercer. *There's a Nightmare in My Closet*. New York: Dial Books for Young Readers, 1968.

Rylant, Cynthia. *The Relatives Came*. New York: Simon & Schuster, 1985.

Speed, Toby. *Two Cool Cows*. New York: G.P. Putnam's Sons, 1995.

Waber, Bernard. *Bearsie Bear and the Surprise Sleepover Party*. New York: Houghton Mifflin Company, 1997.

Zion, Gene. *Harry the Dirty Dog*. New York: Harper & Row, 1956.

MORE BOOKS TO USE FOR COMPOUND WORDS, BLENDS, HOMONYMS, AND SYNONYMS:

Brown, Marc. *Arthur's Teacher Trouble*. Boston: Little, Brown and Company, 1986.

Huck, Charlotte. *Princess Furball*. New York: Greenwillow Books, 1989.

Lionni, Leo. *Frederick*. New York: Alfred A. Knopf, 1967.

Polacco, Patricia. *Thundercake*. New York: Philomel Books, 1990.

Rosen, Michael. *We're Going on a Bear Hunt*. New York: Simon & Schuster, 1989.

Rylant, Cynthia. *When I Was Young in the Mountains*. New York: E.P. Dutton, 1982.

Udry, Janice. *The Moon Jumpers*. New York: Harper & Row Publishers, 1959.

Waber, Bernard. *Funny, Funny Lyle*. Boston: Houghton Mifflin Company, 1987.

MORE BOOKS TO USE FOR VOWELS:

dePaola, Tomie. *Little Grunt and the Big Egg*. New York: Holiday House, Inc., 1990.

Fleming, Denise. *Time to Sleep*. New York: Henry Holt and Company, Inc., 1997.

Kaye, Marilyn. *The Real Tooth Fairy*. New York: Harcourt Brace & Company, 1990.

Kellogg, Steven. *Chicken Little*. New York: Morrow Junior Books, 1985.

Maclachlan, Patricia. *Three Names*. New York: HarperCollins, 1991.

Scieszka, Jon. *The Frog Prince Continued*. New York: Penguin Books, 1991.

———. *The True Story of the Three Little Pigs*. New York: Penguin Books, 1989.

Schwartz, Amy. *Bea and Mr. Jones*. New York: Bradbury Press, 1982.

MORE BOOKS TO USE FOR REVIEWING WORD POWER SKILLS:

Aliki. *Those Summers*. New York: HarperCollins, 1996.

Fleming, Denise. *Lunch*. New York: Henry Holt and Company, Inc., 1992

Henkes, Kevin. *Lilly's Purple Plastic Purse*. New York: Greenwillow Books, 1996.

Pilkey, Dav. *Dogzilla*. New York: Harcourt Brace & Company, 1993.

Steig, William. *Doctor De Soto*. New York: Farrar, Straus and Giroux, 1982.

Schwartz, Amy. *The Purple Coat*. New York: Macmillan Publishing Company, 1992.

Van Allsburg, Chris. *The Polar Express*. Boston: Houghton Mifflin Company, 1985.

Additional Teacher Resources

Johnson, Terry and Daphne Lewis. *Literacy Through Literature*. Portsmouth, NH: Heinemann, 1987.

Routman, Regie. *Invitations: Changing as Teachers and Learners K–12*. Portsmouth, NH: Heinemann, 1991.

—————. *Kids' Poems: Teaching Children to Love Writing Poetry*. New York: Scholastic Professional Books, 2000.